"My dear friend Wendy has trained thousands of women in practical theology through her teaching ministry. I am delighted to see her helpful wisdom now being made available to many more women through this book."

—**Mark Driscoll,** Pastor and Founder, Mars Hill Church;
President, Acts 29 Church Planting Network;
President, Resurgence

Practical **Theology** for Women

How Knowing God Makes a Difference
in Our Daily Lives

Wendy Horger Alsup

CROSSWAY BOOKS

WHEATON, ILLINOIS

Trade Paperback ISBN 978-1-4335-0209-5
PDF ISBN: 978-1-4335-0448-8
Mobipocket ISBN: 978-1-4335-0449-5

Library of Congress Cataloging-in-Publication Data

Alsup, Wendy Horger, 1970–
    Practical theology for women : how knowing God makes a difference in our daily lives /
    Wendy Horger Alsup.
        p. cm.
    Includes index.
    ISBN 978-1-4335-0209-5 (tpb)
    1. Christian women—Religious life. 2. Theology, Practical. I. Title.

    BV4527.A47   2008
    248.8'43—dc22

                                                                            2008005005

VP   16   15   14   13   12   11   10
               9   8   7   6   5   4   3   2

To my husband, Andy,
God's instrument of grace and sanctification in my life—
your wisdom and discernment constantly amaze me.
I love you!

Contents

Part 3: Communicating with Our God

Preface:
Who Am I?

efore we begin our discussion of why women need theology, I want to share with you a little about who I am and what theology has meant to me. My name is Wendy Alsup, and I am actively involved in women's ministry in Seattle, Washington. I am from a relatively small town in the low country of South Carolina. My parents were saved shortly after I was born and were faithful to take us to church every Sunday. I came to understand my need for Jesus at an early age and began my walk with him. During hard times I found comfort, even as a teenager, reading Scripture. God always met me in my need through his Word. Eventually, I headed to Bible college and, afterward, on to graduate school, getting a master's degree in math education.

During the years between college and graduate school, I spent time teaching in South Korea. While there, I developed type-1, insulin-dependent diabetes. It was months before I realized what was going on, and it took another year to figure out how to regulate this condition and regain my health. It was during this time that

God convinced me of the unique power of Scripture to change lives. I was home from Korea, trying to regulate my blood sugars. On one particular day I exercised, meticulously measured what I ate, and took the appropriate amount of insulin—I did everything right. But when I checked my blood sugar that evening, it was very high. I was devastated. I had grown up thinking that sickness was God's judgment on me, and now I thought back on all the ways I had failed God during that day. Based on my understanding of God, having uncontrollable diabetes seemed just retribution for all I had done wrong. I felt condemned.

I managed to crawl over to my one-year Bible (which actually took me three years to read) and found the reading for that day. I wasn't searching for Scripture to make me feel better—I want to emphasize that this was the scheduled reading for that day. It was from John 9:

> As he passed by, he saw a man blind from birth. And his disciples asked him, "Rabbi, who sinned, this man or his parents, that he was born blind?" Jesus answered, "It was not that this man sinned, or his parents, but that the works of God might be displayed in him." (John 9:1–3)

Then Jesus healed the man, giving further evidence of his power as God. I wept as I read this. In that moment I realized his Word is supernatural and living, and it is his means of speaking personally to me as an individual. And from that day on, I never again saw my diabetes as judgment from God. Instead, it was an avenue to bring him glory. I didn't know how he was going to do it, but I trusted from that day on that he was going to use my diabetes for good and not for punishment in my life. This was a radical change to my thinking.

In time, I met my husband, Andy, whom God would use to continue to change my life. I was the good girl who did as I was expected to do. Andy, on the other hand, was a cynic who sometimes got labeled as rebellious. He challenged a lot of the religious traditions I embraced, forcing me to think through why I did what I did. In our first year of marriage, we landed in a rural church pastored by a Reformed evangelical pastor. He preached through Galatians, Ephesians, and Jonah, and something clicked in both our heads. I had known every Bible story from childhood, but they sat in my brain like a filing cabinet full of separate folders. Under this pastor's teaching, I started to see the connections between Jonah and the gospel, between Judges and Jesus Christ. The Scripture stopped being a series of disjointed moral lessons and started being the connected, coherent revelation of the person of Jesus Christ. It was a beautiful time for both Andy and me.

Journey of Faith

In the midst of this time of growth in understanding Scripture, the Lord started working in our hearts, as a couple, about helping a new church in Seattle. After the Lord convinced us that this was his will for us, Andy and I made plans to move from South Carolina to Seattle. This began a two-year journey of faith in which God taught us many things about himself. We made plans, because that's what responsible people do. We counted the cost and had a good perspective on the way we should go. But God had a different path for us to travel, and we seemed thwarted at every turn in our attempts to make it happen.

In particular, despite all his best efforts, Andy couldn't find a job. He went without full-time employment for nearly a year. As the time approached for us to move to Seattle with still no job on the horizon, I came into Sunday evening worship at our rural southern church ready to throw in the towel. Nothing was going right, Andy and I seemed attacked on many different sides, and, simply put, Andy needed a job. I had talked Andy into applying for a job in South Carolina, because I had given up hope of finding a job in Seattle. Then, on that Sunday evening, I walked into church to seek counsel on giving up the whole idea of helping a church in Seattle. I ran into one of our elders before the service. I told him my frustration, and he reminded me that God is faithful, he keeps his promises, and he doesn't lead us to places and then leave us alone to deal with the consequences. Then I ran into another elder and his wife. They told me emphatically not to give up and shared their testimony of how the Lord had used a tough financial time to mold them to his image. I told the wife that I just wanted to fast-forward to the time when this was all over. She told me, "No! The journey is as beautiful as the destination. The trials now, this entire pruning process, are a good thing." Then she recounted the blessing the Lord had worked in their lives through his time of pruning them. Next, I ran into another friend. I told her that the Lord had paid a lot of bills with a little bit of money, but surely it had to run out at some point. Her response was simply, "No, it doesn't."

That little rebuke hit me in the gut. No, the money doesn't have to run out. Yes, the widow's oil lasted until she no longer needed it. The five loaves and two fish fed five thousand plus, and then they had twelve baskets left over. I knew all these Bible stories, so why did I have so little faith? Why couldn't I believe for the long haul that God would meet every need? Why wouldn't I admit confidently with David, "I have been young, and now am old, yet I have not seen the righteous forsaken or his children begging for bread" (Psalm 37:25)? I knew in theory that God does all these things, and yet my knowledge of God was still only just starting to meet me in the practical issues of life.

Eventually, the Lord did provide a great job for Andy in Seattle. But he did it in such a way that we would *never* forget that the job came from his hand. While we were still waiting to hear whether Andy would have a job in Seattle, we had to decide whether to go ahead with the move. We had felt strongly for several years that the Lord wanted us to be involved with church work in Seattle. We sold our house and furniture to get ready for that move and planned to go to Seattle as soon as I finished graduate school. Yet, even after years of responsible planning, when the day came to move we still had no jobs or vehicles or the means by which to get them. Despite our best-laid plans, we were broke, paying rent for a shack in Seattle, and needing to buy a vehicle (though neither of us had any income) in order to haul our things in a trailer across the country.

Since I was in education, we had a small window for moving between the end of graduate school and the beginning of any teaching assignments I might be able to get in Seattle. As the deadline approached for moving, friends and family came to help us load up the car and trailer, which was paid for on credit extended to us by the grace of God. As we drove out of our neighborhood, I felt like I was stepping off the side of a cliff, trusting that in the mist there was something under my feet on which to step. I prayed, as we pulled out of our neighborhood in South Carolina, that God would not allow us to leave the state if he didn't want us in Seattle. We had completely exhausted our cash reserves. This truly was my crisis point. Driving out of South Carolina with all my belongings in an eight-by-ten trailer symbolized walking right off the edge of that cliff.

Two hours later, as we pulled into the Georgia State Welcome Center, Andy got a call from the company that would eventually become his employer in Seattle. They were definitely interested in hiring him and were checking his references. That may not sound like much to you now, but I can't describe how that moment is etched in my memory. All of a sudden, I felt like God rolled back the clouds for a moment and gave me a glimpse of himself I had never seen before. Was that how Abraham felt when he found the ram in the bushes and became the first to call God Jehovah-jireh, God-provider?

How did Elijah feel when God sent down the fire to burn up the altars after they had been doused with bucket after bucket of water? I sobbed the entire time we were at the welcome center, humbled not just by what God had done but also by how he had done it. We caught a glimpse of the splendor of God, his sovereign control over the details of life, and his intimate awareness of our lives. I knew beyond a shadow of a doubt that God wanted us in Seattle and had a definite plan for us. My theology was becoming very practical.

Andy and I basked in the beauty of God's provision of a job for a while. I started a new job as well, teaching math at the local community college. We enjoyed our first few weeks in Seattle, began attending our new church, and got settled into a community group. We had learned profound lessons and thought we had conquered the worst in life by surviving a year of unemployment. Then, six weeks after Andy began his job, we entered the next phase of testing and strengthening.

Tried and Tested

We found out that what we originally thought was asthma was actually a life-threatening heart condition that required immediate surgery for Andy. As Andy, pale-faced with wavering voice, informed me of the prognosis from his doctor's visit, we were both confronted with our need to claim, in that pivotal moment, all we knew about the character of God. Andy was twenty-five years old. We had been married for just a few years. We weren't supposed to be dealing with open-heart surgery at this stage of life.

The morning of Andy's surgery, I had to say good-bye to him at 6:30 AM. The nurses dropped me off in the surgery waiting area before they rolled him into surgery pre-op. I sat in the darkened waiting area completely by myself, stunned and numbed by the enormity of what we were facing. To my surprise, just fifteen minutes later, at 6:45 AM, the first couple from our community group at church walked through the waiting room doors. Kevin was a medical student at the hospital and later had to leave to begin his rounds. His wife, Missy, brought muffins and stayed with me for several hours. More friends, all new acquaintances from community group, came in during the morning. Some had to leave, and new ones came to take their place. At any one time, we probably had at least four people from our church talking and laughing with Andy's parents and me during the entire surgery. After the surgeon finally came out to give us a report, our friends thanked God with us, promised to be back the following day, and went home.

Before I could see Andy, he had to be moved to the cardiothoracic intensive care unit and stabilized. So I went outside the hospital to use my cell phone to call friends and family with the news that he had made it through surgery. As I walked back into the hospital lobby after making my calls, I heard two frantic announcements over the loud speaker for Andy's surgeon to return to the intensive care unit STAT. I knew immediately that something was wrong. What I didn't know was that Andy's heart had stopped, and he had to be revived and taken back in for another open-heart surgery. I was alone in the hospital lobby when I heard the calls to Andy's doctors to return to his side STAT. That was a freakish, surreal moment—I knew that something had gone very wrong by the sound of the announcements, but I went up the wrong elevator at the hospital, and it took a very long time to get to the right place to find out what was happening. The Lord and I had a frank encounter in that lobby as I tried to convince him I couldn't live without Andy, while he reminded me that he is holy, and the outcome of this thing would be good and right for his name's sake. Again, the practical nature of theology became extremely important to me.

By the time I finally found the intensive care unit, Kevin, the medical student from our church, was in the waiting area with

Andy's parents. He too had heard the announcement and was able to go behind the scenes and find out for us what was happening. He let us know the specifics of the problem but protected us from the knowledge of how close Andy was to dying. Later that evening, after Andy was stabilized, one of the pastors from church came by to see us. I had never met him before, but he lived close to the hospital and talked with me for a long time. He gave me his cell phone number and told me to use their home for showers or rest any time. I smiled politely, thanked him, but never considered taking him up on the offer. Honestly, I just didn't know him or his wife well enough to impose on them.

Like a good wife, I planned to spend the nights with Andy. I made it through one night in the hospital, but around 10 PM on the second or third night, Andy's heart got off rhythm. It wasn't incredibly serious, but on top of my sleep deprivation, it sent me over the edge. I humbly fished out the cell phone number for the pastor who lived around the corner from the hospital, though I was formerly too proud to even contemplate inviting myself over. I was barely coherent as I sobbed my need for a place to sleep. He had me walk to their house. It was the night before Thanksgiving. He and his wife put a fire log in the fireplace and made up their sofa bed with lots of comfortable blankets. They made me a cup of tea, put their arms around me, prayed with me, and tucked me into bed.

Lessons Learned

That was an important week in my life theologically. Not only did our church in Seattle constantly meet our needs, but several elders from our church in South Carolina flew out to be with us as well. I finally began to understand the theological concept of the body of Christ. These Christians—the body of Christ in Seattle, Washington, that I barely knew, and the body of Christ in South Carolina that I knew well—were Christ's hands and feet.

They were being exactly what the church is commanded to be in 1 Corinthians 12:24–27:

> But God has combined the members of the body and has given greater honor to the parts that lacked it, so that there should be no division in the body, but that its parts should have equal concern for each other. If one part suffers, every part suffers with it; if one part is honored, every part rejoices with it. Now you are the body of Christ, and each one of you is a part of it. (NIV)

When my personal pride threatened to curb my willingness to accept help, the Lord reminded me of Matthew 25:35–40:

> "'For I was hungry and you gave me food, I was thirsty and you gave me drink, I was a stranger and you welcomed me, I was naked and you clothed me, I was sick and you visited me, I was in prison and you came to me.' Then the righteous will answer him, saying, 'Lord, when did we see you hungry and feed you, or thirsty and give you drink? And when did we see you a stranger and welcome you, or naked and clothe you? And when did we see you sick or in prison and visit you?' And the King will answer them, 'Truly, I say to you, as you did it to one of the least of these my brothers, you did it to me.'"

Each gift of coffee and muffins, each offer of a meal or errand run, each dish washed and cycle of laundry done for me, all of these were ministries directly to Christ as well as to me. It was neat to meditate on the mystery of Matthew 25 as I watched the body of Christ serve Andy and me over and over again.

As only God can do, the months of sickness, worry, and recovery actually were a very sweet time for our marriage. By the time Andy had recovered from that surgery, we were well convinced of God's uncanny ability to turn horrible circumstances into precious treasures. The process of learning to trust God continued as we miscarried our first child a few months later and entered a season of infertility. Once again, our brothers and sisters in Christ ministered to us in ways that revealed precious glimpses of God's character and splendor. Looking back at those trials, I am reminded of the truth of God's character that I so often forget. Our trials, though painful for us, brought about wonderful fruit in our lives. Like Moses in Exodus 33, we caught a glimpse of God's glory, and it was the most beautiful thing we have ever seen.

Before moving to Seattle, we had the novel idea that we wanted to help start a church that would communicate sound theology in a culturally relevant way. Then we stumbled upon one and realized God was well ahead of us in that plan. I began volunteering there shortly after we moved to Seattle and continued throughout Andy's convalescence. The church intrigued me. It looked like a well-oiled machine from the outside, and I wondered about its secret to success. I soon learned there was no magic formula. I found a group of humble servants who believed Scripture, submitted to the Holy Spirit, and willingly endured the chaos that followed. During this time I got to know two deacons, who later became elders. After several months of conversations with them, we began to sense the Spirit leading me toward a leadership role in our loosely organized women's ministry. In time, I became deacon of women's theology and teaching.

Those months of volunteering in the church office were of immense value to me. I had walked into the church thinking I had something to offer them. After all, I was raised in the church and had even attended Bible college. After listing my spiritual résumé to the office staff, they nodded politely and stuck me in a windowless room filling out bank deposit slips by myself. It was humbling that they didn't immediately ask me to counsel women or teach a class. But they had enough experience with so-called mature Christians to know I needed a season of testing. They gave me a job that I couldn't ruin through a personal agenda. That allowed me to come to a better understanding of the church culture and allowed church leadership to get to know me. I needed that time to get to know the people of Seattle to which our church ministered. It was a culture that was very different from the one in which I was raised. I learned during this time to shut my mouth and listen to the ideas of others instead of projecting my preconceived notions onto them.

In my years of listening to the women here, I have come to dearly love and respect their stories of redemption and transformation. My sisters in Christ fit no stereotype. Purple hair, nose rings, and tattoos aside, our women have a variety of backgrounds, interests, and struggles. But their lives testify consistently of the power of the gospel to radically transform lives. One woman in a class I recently taught first came to church to rescue her boyfriend from our church, which she thought of as "this cult." He had come home after attending a service and informed her they could no longer sleep together. This local college student figured if she listened to the preaching for a few weeks, she could eventually disprove the pastor. Instead, she came to Christ, went through our gospel class, and ended up in the Practical Theology for Women class. Now she and her boyfriend are married, growing in Christ, and preparing for future ministry. Her testimony is just one of many. God has shown his power to radically transform lives again and again through the women of this church.

I thank God daily for the gift of ministry he has given me in my church and home. God has called me to be a wise and prudent helper to my husband (Genesis 2:18; Proverbs 19:14) and a faithful mother to my boys. I am often tempted to find my identity and value in ministry outside my house, but God regularly reminds me that finding my identity and value in anything other than him is idolatry. I seek to be a good steward of my ministries in the order of priority God has set—husband, children, and then outside ministry. My husband highly values my opinion, but when we disagree, I willingly submit to him (Ephesians 5:22–33). I love our elders and submit to their leadership as well.

As you will see in the following chapters, it is my deepest conviction that what God teaches about himself in his Word is of utmost importance to the issues of my personal daily life. That's the heart of my ministry to women. As you read this book, I hope you too catch the vision of the power of theology to transform us as women where it counts most.

Part *One*

What Is Theology?

What exactly is *Practical Theology for Women*? As a starting point for this discussion, I'll use a conversation I had with a friend one Sunday afternoon when we talked about what we were learning at our respective churches. When I brought up a doctrinal issue my pastor had mentioned in his message, my friend, who attended another good church in our town, said to me that she studies the Bible only for its practical application and avoids getting involved in discussions of the deep things of the Word of God. She did not feel it was wise for her personally to dive too deeply into the Bible. She simply wanted a "thought for the day" from her Bible reading, kind of like a cheesy Christian desk calendar. During our conversation, I realized that she, like many Christians, viewed the Bible as two separate tracks—the simple, practical, everyday application stuff for the average Christian, and another, perhaps higher, level of spiritual study reserved for pastors and seminary graduates. While that may reflect what we see playing out in the church today, it is *not* a biblical concept.

Perhaps you ask, why write a theology book specifically geared toward women? Is this theology different from what should be in a book for men? Absolutely not! But for some reason, most theology books are written by men and aimed at a predominantly male audience. With this book, I hope to fight the unspoken mentality that theology is for men, while parenting, sewing, or dieting classes are for women. I have heard some women argue that they don't want to know more theology than their husbands know. They seem to fear that studying theology will turn them into theological Amazon queens who naturally relegate their husbands to some second-class position in the home. But this is a terrible way to think about theology. God forbid that women should avoid studying the deep things of the Word lest they surpass the understanding of the men in their lives! Studying theology—such as the Holy Spirit's role in convicting man of sin, and God's sovereignty over all creation—will curb, not enhance, a woman's sinful tendency to nag and manipulate her husband. My husband can bear witness to the fact that a better understanding of God's character, that is, theology, makes me a better wife. No matter where our husbands, fathers, or pastors may be in their spiritual journey, when we ladies grow in our understanding of God's character and attributes, it can only be a blessing for our homes, our marriages, and our churches.

1

Why Should I Care?

According to *The American Heritage Dictionary of the English Language, theology* is defined in three ways:

1) The study of the nature of God and religious truth.
2) A system or school of opinions concerning God and religious questions: *Protestant theology; Jewish theology.*
3) A course of specialized religious study usually at a college or seminary.[1]

The definition begins by stating that theology is "the study of the nature of God." However, many Christians perceive theology as just part 3 of the definition—"a course of specialized religious study usually at a college or seminary." Is that what the study of

God should be? Should the study of God and deep religious truth be restricted to the academic elite at colleges and seminaries? Why do so many Christians believe that theology is a special topic for a select few in the body of Christ and not meant for the average man or woman sitting in a church pew?

No one can say for sure why so many Christians (like my friend whom I mentioned in the introduction) are content for the pastors and elders of a church to be the keepers of the deep knowledge of God, so long as they pass along a practical tidbit each week to help the average church attendee through his daily life. Perhaps the key is that Christians today often believe that the deep things of God—doctrine and theology—are not practical, and that the practical things of the Bible are not deep. But this type of thinking flies in the face of simple biblical principles, two of which we'll look at now.

Knowing God Is Practical

"The fear of the LORD is the beginning of wisdom, and the knowledge of the Holy One is insight" (Prov. 9:10). Most church attendees admit that they need wisdom. Each Sunday many come to church hoping for the preacher to give some principle that they can apply to their lives in the coming week that will make them a wiser parent, spouse, employer, or employee. Proverbs 9:10 holds the answer. The Bible repeatedly says that wisdom in practical daily living is preceded by "the fear of the LORD" and "the knowledge of the Holy One."

> "And he said to man,
>   'Behold, the fear of the Lord, that is wisdom,
>   and to turn away from evil is understanding.'"
>   (Job 28:28)

> The fear of the LORD is the beginning of wisdom;
>> all those who practice it have a good understanding.
>> His praise endures forever! (Psalm 111:10)

> The fear of the LORD is instruction in wisdom,
>> and humility comes before honor. (Proverbs 15:33)

It's obvious from these Scriptures that wise, practical daily living is preceded by a knowledge of God that leads to fear, awe, and reverence of him, his power, and his purposes. In other words, *theology is the root, foundation, and framework for practical living that reflects wisdom and understanding.*

Christ Is Our High Priest

"For there is one God, and there is one mediator between God and men, the man Christ Jesus" (1 Timothy 2:5).

I'll sum up the second biblical principle on the importance of theology with the phrase "the priesthood of Christ." Hang with me while I explain. In the Old Testament, God set up a system for entering into his presence in the temple. His dwelling place was called the Most Holy Place and was separated from the rest of the temple by a heavy veil or curtain. Once a year, only the high priest could pass through the veil and enter the Most Holy Place. This high priest was the mediator or middleman between the average Jew, who remained in the outer part of the temple, and God, who dwelled in the Most Holy Place. Before entering the Most Holy Place, however, the high priest was required to offer a blood sacrifice "for himself and for the unintentional sins of the people" (Hebrews 9:7).

In the new covenant (New Testament), Jesus Christ has become our great High Priest. Hebrews 8–10 tells us that Christ's death on the cross satisfied the penalty for the sins of mankind. His death fulfilled the bloody sacrificial system, making Christ the final perfect sacrifice for the sins of mankind. Rather than doing away with the Old Testament system, he fulfilled it (see Matthew 5:17–20). Now, Christ is the mediator—the middleman between all Christian believers and God. Hebrews 10:19–22 reveals the implications of this truth:

> Therefore, brothers, since we have confidence to enter the holy places by the blood of Jesus, by the new and living way that he opened for us through the curtain, that is, through his flesh, and since we have a great priest over the house of God, let us draw near with a true heart in full assurance of faith, with our hearts sprinkled clean from an evil conscience and our bodies washed with pure water.

Through Christ, each of us has access to God's throne room and can boldly draw near to God in full assurance of faith. Upon salvation, we have Christ as our mediator and intercessor before God. He is our High Priest. We are not dependent upon another priest, pastor, the Virgin Mary, or any other spiritual authority figure to intercede on our behalf before God. If you know Christ as your Savior, you have the same Holy Spirit residing in your heart, the same Word of God at your fingertips, and the same access to the presence of God as the wisest and most godly spiritual leader you know of today. It's a copout to leave the deep things of God to the pastors and seminary graduates when, in Christ, we have the same access to God that they do. That was never what God intended.

Seek God

Don't be content with the Christian desk calendar approach to Christianity. Don't be satisfied with a daily practical saying or some three-step process for being a good wife or a better friend. God has both called you and equipped you to know him. We have no excuse to remain ignorant of his character. Seek God's face. Understand his character. Pursue knowledge of him, for apart from the "fear of the Lord" and "the knowledge of the Holy One" (Proverbs 9:10) we have no hope for being a wise mother, sister, wife, or friend.

So, what is theology and why should I care? Theology is basically just the study of God—who he is and what he does. Proverbs says that such knowledge of God is the foundation for wise living. So we study theology that we may know God and be enlightened to the benefits of our relationship with him. This is a supernatural journey with God. As Paul prays for believers in Ephesians 1:17–20, we are dependent on God our Father to give us "a spirit of wisdom and of revelation in the knowledge of him," that we may "know what is the hope to which he has called [us], what are the riches of his glorious inheritance in the saints, and what is the immeasurable greatness of his power toward us who believe." I hope you will adopt this as your prayer as well, for you cannot unlock this on your own.

Paul goes on to explain that the same power that raised Christ from the dead is the power at work in us who believe. So our journey now, in prayer to God and study of his Word, begins with learning of his character and work and then examining our lives to see if our responses daily reflect belief in our glorious inheritance in him. This leads us into the next chapter.

2

What Is Faith?

We walk by faith, not by sight.

—2 Corinthians 5:7

 once heard an interesting story concerning Vince Lombardi's strategy for coaching his football team. Each season at spring training, the legendary coach would begin the first team meeting by reviewing the fundamental concepts of the game—starting simply with the football. Perhaps he found that his team tended to get so caught up in the details of their positions and plays that they lost sight of the fundamental procedures and goals of the game. In a similar fashion, many Christians focus so much on the minute details of their problems that they lose sight of the fundamental concepts that govern life for a believer in Christ. This chapter focuses on one of those fundamental concepts—possibly the most important concept in all of Scripture—faith.

29

Lessons of Faith

God has taught my family hard lessons on faith over the last few years. The most intense lessons came when the Lord moved us from South Carolina to Seattle, Washington, which I recounted in the preface of this book. At the time of our move, my husband had been unemployed for nearly a year. After the end of that year of unemployment and the upheaval of moving across the country to a new home, my young husband was diagnosed with a heart condition that called for an immediate open-heart surgery. The initial surgery was fairly successful, but his heart stopped later that afternoon. He was revived, and after a second surgery that day, a week in the intensive care unit, and another week battling pneumonia at the local medical center, he finally made a full recovery. The Lord used those circumstances to work on both of us, a young married couple, in a very intense way, testing and molding our faith in him beyond anything we had experienced before.

That series of trials provided a number of opportunities for me to observe my husband, our families, our friends, and myself as we responded to both positive and negative circumstances affecting our lives. I began to notice a disconcerting disconnect between what some Christians said they believed and how they acted, and I began to contemplate these things. What enables one man to face open-heart surgery with calm assurance, while another man is devastated because his car's transmission needs to be overhauled? What force drives one woman to near hysterics as she contemplates flying in a plane, while another woman seeks to encourage her family even as she shares the news that she has breast cancer? As believers, we expect those who don't know Christ to react to negative circumstances with fear and worry. But does it fit with our belief system when such reactions characterize those who claim to believe in Christ and trust in his Word?

Let's study what the Bible says about faith, starting with the "faith chapter" in Hebrews 11. After we've defined faith from Scripture, we'll survey Scripture's examples of people who lacked faith and follow up with passages that give us evidences of genuine faith. What we'll see in Scripture is that true faith definitely plays out practically in a believer's life. The goal in this part of our study is to remove any disconnect between what we *say* we believe and what our *actions* show our true beliefs to be. Faith in Christ is a very practical piece of theology. To say we have faith in him while living a life characterized by anxiety and worry is to deny him by our actions, if not our words.

Hebrews 11 and Faith

What exactly is faith? We are told in Hebrews 11:6 that "without faith it is impossible to please God" (NIV). If there is no way to please God apart from faith, then we must understand what faith is and what faith is not. Rather than defining the term myself, I'm going to rely on the Bible's own definition of the term:

> Now faith is being sure of what we hope for and certain of what we do not see. This is what the ancients were commended for. By faith we understand that the universe was formed at God's command, so that what is seen was not made out of what was visible. By faith Abel offered God a better sacrifice than Cain did. By faith he was commended as a righteous man, when God spoke well of his offerings. And by faith he still speaks, even though he is dead. By faith Enoch was taken from this life, so that he did not experience death; he could not be found, because God had taken him away. For before he was taken, he was commended as one who pleased God. And without faith it is impossible to please God, because anyone who comes to him must believe that he exists and that he rewards those who earnestly seek him. (Hebrews 11:1–6 NIV)

31

According to verse one, faith is being sure of what we hope for and certain of what we do not see. And it is for this surety that the ancients, the Old Testament characters mentioned in this passage, are commended. They were sure. They were certain. They were confident. But sure about what? Certain of what?

The answer is in verse 6. Anyone who comes to God must believe that "he exists" and that "he rewards those who earnestly seek him." "He exists" alludes to a special name God used to reveal himself, "I AM." God first refers to himself as "I AM" in Exodus 3: "God said to Moses, 'I AM WHO I AM'; and He said, 'Thus you shall say to the sons of Israel, "I AM has sent me to you"'" (Exodus 3:14 NASB).

The Hebrew word translated "LORD" in the Old Testament is "YHWH," meaning "the existing one."[1] It is based on the same word, *Hâyâh*, that is translated "I AM" in Exodus 3:14.[2] Although I grew up in the church, I was well into adulthood before I really began contemplating the meaning of God's name, "I AM."

"I am."

"I exist."

"I am real."

It's not crazy for us to doubt much of what we experience in life. A little skepticism can be quite healthy, but we must have no doubt whatsoever about God and his existence. He is! The issue here is not what he is. It is enough simply that he exists.

God's existence alone makes the rest of life's inconveniences and struggles fade in comparison. I have often had to focus on this concept when facing difficult situations. I remember a particular time when I was driving home after a frustrating day at my new teaching assignment. I wondered how I ended up in that place and what I should do about it. I was stressed, discouraged, and anxious. All at once, I remembered him. My anxiety faded as I meditated on the fact that he is. He is real. He is trustworthy. He is in control. He is, he is, he is. Your job may not be _____ (fill in the blank), but your God exists and he is real.

Many Christians in today's churches seem much more convinced of the reality of their problems than the reality of their God. Our cell phone bill, the transmission in our car, or the coworker in the next cubicle consumes our thoughts. Whether we are single or married, stay-at-home moms or working women, we tend to get so tied up in the minutiae of life that we miss the biggest truth, the ultimate reality. God must be big in our minds. God needs to be at the forefront of our thought processes. He needs to be the first consideration in all of our daily circumstances, not the last resort that we consider after exhausting all other options. Believing in his existence—focusing with trust on his reality—is fundamental to a faith that pleases God.

God is, and his existence alone puts the rest of life in perspective. The extension of this concept is to ask, "God is—what?" Colossians 1 and Hebrews 1 show us exactly who and what he is:

> [Jesus] is the image of the invisible God, the firstborn of all creation. For by him all things were created, in heaven and on earth, visible and invisible, whether thrones or dominions or rulers or authorities—all things were created through him and for him. And he is before all things, and in him all things hold together. And he is the head of the body, the church. He is the beginning, the firstborn from the dead, that in everything he might be preeminent. For in him all the fullness of God was pleased to dwell, and through him to reconcile to himself all things, whether on earth or in heaven, making peace by the blood of his cross. (Colossians 1:15–20)

> God, after He spoke long ago to the fathers in the prophets in many portions and in many ways, in these last days has spoken to us in His Son. . . . And He is the radiance of His glory and the exact representation of His nature. (Hebrews 1:1–3 NASB)

These passages present Jesus as God who came to live among us to show us his glory firsthand. In Colossians 1, Paul teaches that Christ is the image of the invisible God, and through Christ all things hold together. According to Hebrews 1, Jesus Christ is the exact representation of God's nature. Christ is our formerly invisible God who came to live among us so that we may know exactly who he is. Furthermore, he is the one who holds all the issues of our daily lives together. By him all things consist. If you want to know God, you must know Jesus Christ. We'll explore Jesus in more depth in chapters 10 and 11.

The Rewards of Faith

According to Hebrews 11:6, the first aspect of faith is our firm conviction of God's existence. The other facet of faith is the belief that "he rewards those who seek him." That sounds easy enough, yet many Christians live their lives acting as if God is the big bully in the sky. I have watched friends hide as unobtrusively as possible lest they draw God's attention, fearful that he might catch their eye and ask of them some horrid act of sacrifice. Many of you can identify with them. You sit in church services singing the alphabet song with your fingers in your ears, desperately trying to avoid conviction to do anything that pulls you out of your comfort zone. I know one friend who was reading a book about walking deeper with Jesus. The author made a comment along the lines of "don't read any farther if you don't want to be challenged in your faith." My friend said she put the book down right then. She believed God exists. But she thinks he lives to ask hard things of the people who follow him too closely. Whatever rewards he promises for those who diligently seek him are not nearly enough to warrant her trust in him. Very few of us would admit we think of God this way, but if we examine ourselves, we notice that our actions often contradict our words.

Let's be honest with ourselves and God. Do you understand what it means that God rewards those who seek him? Does it mean that he gives believers nice consolation prizes after they've given up their money, families, and comforts to serve him in the darkest corner of Africa? Do you think the rewards are at best pats on the back or small tokens of affection to make up for all the sacrifices? If so, then no wonder you are afraid to get close to him! You think the rewards aren't worth the sacrifices. At least admit it to yourself—you have a small view of God and his promises.

When you hear of someone talking about knowing God better, are you inspired? One woman told me she already knew all there was to know about God. What? Are you kidding me? She might as well claim that she knows all there is to know about the universe. But there she sits, oblivious to all she doesn't know about him and content in her ignorance. Do you realize he is bigger, deeper, and better than we have the ability to comprehend? And he wants us to know things about him that pass our ability to understand on our own, to know the love that surpasses knowledge (Ephesians 3:19). Understanding him changes us in glorious ways.

Part of the problem with discussing the meaning of the rewards of Hebrews 11:6 is that they are very hard to explain until you have experienced them firsthand. How can you explain to someone that you would not trade your year of unemployment and financial concerns for anything in the world because the beauty of God's provision so richly outweighed the struggle? Who would believe that your young husband's heart surgery was worth it—truly worth every ounce of pain—because God opened your eyes to something so incredibly beautiful about himself that it defies explanation?

This is what Abraham experienced after he climbed the mountain to sacrifice his son Isaac in Genesis 22. Before he climbed that mountain, he did not know that God would provide a substitute with the ram in the bushes. God had never been called Jehovah-jireh (God-provider) in Scripture before that point. Abraham came to know God as Jehovah-jireh on that mountain, learning something precious about God as he held the knife above his son. The blessing that followed that terrible trial, that sweet knowledge of God that has sustained many believers since, was well worth the pain and struggle Abraham endured to learn the lesson.

God's Love

Romans 8:28 sums up the issue this way: "We know that for those who love God all things work together for good, for those who are called according to his purpose." That's a pretty straightforward promise. But reading that verse in its context gives us a little more insight into God's plan. Paul goes on to tell us that "those whom he foreknew he also predestined to be conformed to the image of his Son, in order that he might be the firstborn among many brothers" (v. 29). God's plan before the beginning of time was for his children to be conformed to the likeness of Jesus Christ. This truth is discussed in Colossians 1:28 and Ephesians 4:11–13. It is also emphasized in 2 Corinthians 3:18: "We all, with unveiled face, beholding the glory of the Lord, are being transformed into the same image from one degree of glory to another. For this comes from the Lord who is the Spirit."

We have God's precious promise that he's going to work the hard things in our lives for our good, and part of that good is that we will be changed more and more to reflect Christ's character and glory. The trials and struggles we experience are like the refiner's fire under a pot of gold. The heat brings impurities to the top to be scraped off by the refiner, leaving the gold in a purer form. When God heats up our lives, working out our pride, selfishness, and general wrong thinking, the resulting purified life is so much sweeter. After several intense struggles in my own life, I regularly thank the Lord for the trials and the changes he has wrought in my heart. He has changed my thought processes to ones that more accurately reflect him. With that wonderful, freeing result, I can't help but praise him for the trial.

A second thing revealed to us in Romans 8 is that nothing can separate us from God's love. Our trials come from God's loving hand and are consistent with his love for us.

> What then shall we say to these things? If God is for us, who can be against us? He who did not spare his own Son but gave him up for us all, how will he not also with him graciously give us all things? . . . Who shall separate us from the love of Christ? . . . For I am sure that neither death nor life, nor angels nor rulers, nor things present nor things to come, nor powers, nor height nor depth, nor anything else in all creation, will be able to separate us from the love of God in Christ Jesus our Lord. (Romans 8:31–32, 35, 38–39)

The Bible repeatedly reminds us of God's faithful love. Jeremiah 31:3; 1 John 4:10–16; John 15:12–13; and Deuteronomy 7:7–8 all contain promises concerning his love. When we face uncertain times, we must sift our responses through the filter of this truth. Do I believe that God is working the hard things in my life for my good because he loves me? Do I respond to trials as if God is the big bully in the sky? Or does my response reflect that, despite outward appearances, I believe God loves me and has a good plan for my life?

My responses of unbelief generally fall into two categories. First, I respond in unbelief by taking things into my own hands. I come up with an agenda to fix my situation, usually forgetting God entirely. I start manipulating circumstances in subtle ways or grab the reigns in an obvious effort to regain control and change direction. When God finally gets my attention, I realize that acting in belief usually requires me to put aside my agenda and wait patiently for God to work on my behalf.

My other response of unbelief is despair. When this happens, although I am well aware that God exists, I just no longer believe he's working for my good. Since I can't figure out how God is going to use this bad circumstance for my good, I assume it is impossible that he will. The move from unbelief to belief, in this situation, is evidenced when I move from despair to peace, despite nothing changing in my circumstances. Then I again find myself waiting, but this time I have earnest expectation that God is working this bad situation for my good in ways I am currently unable to comprehend.

Throughout the Bible we see examples of God's using bad things for good in the lives of his children. This is the great paradox of Scripture. The idea of bad things being used by God for good is addressed in different ways throughout Scripture. Christ sums up the paradox using this phrase: "Whoever loses his life for my sake will find it" (Matthew 10:39b; cf. Matthew 10:37–39a; 16:24–25; Mark 8:35; Luke 9:24; 17:33; John 12:25). The psalmist addresses God's supernatural use of bad for good this way: "Because your steadfast love is better than life, my lips will praise you" (Psalm 63:3). The apostle Paul states it yet another way in Galatians 2:20. He writes, "I have been crucified with Christ. It is no longer I who live, but Christ who lives in me. And the life I now live in the flesh I live by faith in the Son of God, who loved me and gave himself for me."

One of my favorite Christian songs is "Crucified with Christ," by Phillips, Craig & Dean. It centers on Paul's words in Galatians 2:20 and begins with the words, "When I look back at what I thought was living, I'm amazed at the price I chose to pay." When it comes down to it, apart from Christ we have very warped views of what the abundant life is all about. Like those songwriters, we pursue our perception of the good life and miss the infinite, sustaining blessings in life that God has for us. Outside of Scripture, no one words this quite as well as C. S. Lewis in *The Weight of Glory*, where he says, "We are half-hearted creatures, fooling about with drink and sex and ambition when infinite joy is offered us, like an ignorant child who wants to go on making mud pies in a slum because he cannot imagine what is meant by the offer of a holiday at the sea. We are far too easily pleased."[3]

God had to take away a lot of things from me before I finally realized that my perspective on the "good life" was all wrong. I never experienced true, abundant living until Christ started taking away the superficial things from me and replacing them with the kind of peace, humility, and security that come only from a deep, abiding relationship with him. I have had many women give testimony to me about how the Lord took away a job, a fiancé, a home, or whatever and used that trial to give them immeasurable blessings through himself. He doesn't ask the same things of any two people, and the struggles he allows into your life will be intensely personal. But when they come, ask yourself, "What is it I believe about God?" Do you believe that he is good? Do you believe his promise to work the hard things for good in your life? Do you trust that he's acting consistently with his claims of love for you? Simply put, do you believe him? And in that dark moment, are you going to let your belief in his goodness or your despair over your struggle lead you? Truly, those who lose their lives in the arms of God's grace are the ones who finally see what true living really is.

In summary, Hebrews 11:6 says that it is impossible to please God without faith. It teaches that authentic faith consists of a confident assurance of God's existence and a confident expectation of his goodness to his children. Now let's look at examples of what faith is and what faith is not from the Old and New Testaments. This survey of Scripture's examples of faith should give us a solid framework for examining our own lives.

3

Faith Works!

Let us fix our eyes on Jesus,
the author and perfecter of our faith,
who for the joy set before him endured the cross,
scorning its shame,
and sat down at the right hand of the throne of God.

—Hebrews 12:2 (NIV)

Who in your life do you consider to be a man or woman of faith? Who in Scripture stands out as an example of faith to you? Think about it for a moment. What is it about them that demonstrates authentic faith to you? Is it what they said? Is it what they did? What have you noticed about how they responded to trials and struggles in their lives?

Unfaithfulness in the Old Testament
Let's start our survey of faith with Old Testament passages dealing with actions that give evidence of a lack of faith. The Hebrew

word *ma'al* is the root behind the Old Testament words *unfaithful,* *unfaithfully,* and *unfaithfulness.* It is also translated "falsehood," "treachery," "trespass," and "broke faith."[1]

Ma'al is used several times in Leviticus and Numbers to give a warning for the consequences of unfaithfulness. In Leviticus and Numbers, the act of unfaithfulness is closely associated with sin:

If a person acts unfaithfully and sins . . . (Leviticus 5:15 NASB)

When a person sins and acts unfaithfully against the LORD . . . (Leviticus 6:2 NASB)

When a man or woman commits any of the sins of mankind, acting unfaithfully against the LORD . . . (Numbers 5:6 NASB)

Later in the Old Testament, *ma'al* is used to describe acts of unfaithfulness. This includes Moses' disobedience at the waters of Meribah-kadesh, where he struck the rock instead of speaking to it in direct violation of God's instructions (see Deuteronomy 32:51). In Joshua 7, *ma'al* describes Achan's unfaithful act of disobedience, plundering the forbidden spoils of war, which leads to his severe punishment, death by stoning. I find both these discussions of unfaithfulness especially interesting (and a bit disconcerting) because both passages are more focused on describing the act of unfaithfulness and God's response than they are on initially setting up the situation.

In the instance of Moses' disobedience, which had very serious consequences, my initial reaction was "what's so bad about hitting the rock?" As I think through that situation, it occurs to me that I have hit rocks a number of times in my life. I can say boldly that I do not have any conviction against hitting rocks and have never heard any pastor preach against hitting rocks. But for Moses, there was something about hitting this particular rock that caused God to accuse him of breaking faith with him and not treating him as holy in front of the children of Israel.

This reminds me that God asked very different acts of faith from different Bible characters. For Abraham, acting faithfully with God involved a willingness to sacrifice his son. For Moses, such an act would have been murder. For Daniel, faithfulness meant refusing the king's meat and drink, but there is no evidence that the same was required for Joseph, another captive of a foreign government. Many people have hit rocks—a good number of those have hit rocks out of anger. However, there was a specific understanding about this particular rock between Moses and God that caused God to rebuke Moses for the unfaithfulness inherent in the action of hitting it.

Even if I had been standing by Moses that day in Meribah-kadesh, I probably wouldn't have understood why hitting that rock caused him to lose the opportunity to lead the Israelites into the Promised Land. But I guarantee that Moses understood. Moses was at a crossroads, and in that moment, he chose to turn his back on what he knew about God—an act of treachery that God strongly rebuked.

I think this marks the first key in unlocking our personal problems with faith. Acts of faith, the practical steps that result from confidence in God's working in our lives, stem from a relationship with God that is real and personal. I have talked with many women who, deep down in that private inner place that only they and God know about, are afraid of the kind of personal relationship with God that might result in him requiring something special from them. They would rather not know God that well. Are you there? Do you psychologically hide from God, singing the alphabet song with your fingers in your ears in an effort to avoid hearing that still, small voice that may call you to take a step of—*gasp*—faith? If so, would you acknowledge with me that this is a serious problem?

Do you find it disturbing to read about the link between a lack of faith and sin? Would you rather think of your lack of faith as a weakness? Personally, it's easier for me to think that it is just a natural reaction to doubt God when circumstances look bleak; but to call it *sin*? That seems awfully harsh. And yet, that's exactly what God calls it; he even calls it treachery—sin with an accompanying stab in the back.

Unfaithfulness in the New Testament

Christ uses the phrase "you of little faith" repeatedly in the New Testament. In our quest to understand faith, it would be wise for us to consider each of the situations where Christ described someone as having "little faith." The word Christ uses is *oligopistos*,[2] meaning "of little faith" or "trusting too little." It comes from *oligos*, meaning simply "little," "small," or "few," and *pistos*, whose meaning deserves consideration. Between the King James Version and the New American Standard Version, *pistos* is translated "assurance," "belief," "faith," "faithfulness," "fidelity," "pledge," and "proof." It implies conviction of the truth of anything. It also implies faithfulness or character that can be relied upon. By combining *oligos* and *pistos* we get the idea of having little conviction of the truth of something or someone.

Jesus first uses *oligopistos* in Matthew 6:30–31 during his discussion about anxiety in the Sermon on the Mount:

> If that is how God clothes the grass of the field, which is here today and tomorrow is thrown into the fire, will he not much more clothe you, O you of little faith? So do not worry, saying, "What shall we eat?" or "What shall we drink?" or "What shall we wear?" (NIV)

In this instance, Christ does not seem to be addressing a particular person's actions. Instead, his words are part of a long discussion on worry and anxiety. Did you notice how he links the state of having little faith with the action of worry? This is key to understanding faith and overcoming worry. Faith is the theological concept. Worry and anxiety are the practical issues of life. Here is clear evidence that the practical issue of worry in our lives is intensely affected by our theology. We cannot separate the two.

In Matthew 8, Christ uses *oligopistos* again. Jesus is asleep on a boat in the middle of a raging storm. His disciples cry frantically to him, "Save us, Lord; we are perishing." Jesus responds, "Why are you afraid, O you of little faith?" (Matthew 8:25–26). This rebuke comes not because they ran to him with their problem, but because they greatly feared the outcome. Their fear was the practical effect of their lack of faith.

The disciples' response here is particularly interesting because they have just witnessed Christ heal a leper, a centurion's servant, Peter's mother-in-law, and several others from an unnamed group. By now they should have a little more confidence in him than they are demonstrating. For an even clearer example of this cycle of Christ's provision and his disciples' forgetfulness, consider Matthew 16. In the chapter just before, Jesus feeds over four thousand people with seven loaves of bread and a few small fish. The disciples not only witness this, but they also give the food to the people and gather the remaining baskets of food. On top of that, this is the second time Christ has performed such a miracle in front of them. Yet they forget the miracle so fast that it would make me laugh if it weren't so pathetic. When the disciples begin discussing, in Matthew 16, that they have no bread, they are once again rebuked by Christ with *oligopistos*, "You of little faith" (v. 18). If you read Christ's rebuke in context, it's hard to put your finger on exactly what aspect of their response marked a lack of faith, but it's clear that they had forgotten something very important that they should have remembered from the previous provisions of food. We see this problem of provision and forgetfulness over and over throughout the Old and New Testaments—and over and over in our own lives. God does something big, and we simply forget. We forget that he provided for us last time. We forget that he worked things together so well for us to get our last job, buy our last house, have our last child. We worry and fret over new problems when we really should know better. The problem is not that we have never seen God provide for us before. The problem is not that he's asking us to respond in a way that is radically different from previous situations; the problem is that we forget the ways he's proven himself in the past and fret over how we are going to provide for ourselves in the new situation. Exhibiting little conviction in the truth of God's promises is especially troublesome when he's proven himself faithful so many times before.

Sometimes the issues are big. Sometimes the issues are small. But, in my case, no matter how many times God has proven himself faithful, it seems my initial reaction to any new problem is fear and anxiety. I have to fight each time to bring my responses back into line with what I know about him. Recently I had a misunderstanding with a dear friend, which caused me a lot of distress. After a few hours I began seeking God on how to respond in a way that would reflect the gospel and what I know to be true about God's character. When my friend and I next talked, God allowed us to resolve my concern without conflict.

But then, two days later, a similar conflict arose. Instead of thinking immediately of all God had shown me about himself earlier in the week, my first response was anger and bitterness that such a conflict was happening again. After a few hours of forgetting God, I began to remember what I know of him and how a few days before he had shown his ability to reconcile conflict. Once again, after taking my thoughts captive and making them submit to what I knew to be true about God, God resolved this conflict in a way that actually strengthened our friendship.

But so often, just like the Israelites in the Old Testament and the disciples in the New Testament, I completely forget all the ways God has shown himself faithful to me and others throughout time. Due to such forgetfulness, God instructed the Israelites to put up markers at places where God had done something mighty for them. Similarly, in light of my forgetfulness, I find journaling to be a helpful tool for remembering God's work in my life.

Faithfulness in the Scriptures

In contrast to the previous section, let's consider examples of faithfulness from Scripture. Consider Christ's words in Matthew 8 describing the centurion who came to him. Jesus says, "I tell you, with no one in Israel have I found such faith" (Matthew 8:10). Once again, the word used for "faith" here is *pistis*, meaning "conviction of the truth" and "belief resulting in trust." The centurion came to Jesus, asking him to heal his servant. When Jesus moved to go to the man's house, the centurion said, "Lord, I am not worthy to have you come under my roof, but only say the word, and my servant will be healed" (v. 8). In effect, he was saying, "Lord, I don't need to see it. You can just say it right here, and I'll trust you and walk home by myself confident all the way that you healed my servant—even though I haven't seen the results." This man believed Christ, and it showed in how he responded.

I am blessed by this man's example. He didn't verbally announce his belief in Christ. Instead he lived his belief in Christ. He walked up to Christ, not with confidence in himself but with an absolute, unshakeable confidence in Jesus Christ. I love the fact that Jesus was "astonished" by his response (v. 10 NIV). Jesus was repeatedly gracious with those whose faith wavered, and I am so thankful that he continues to be gracious with his children today. Oh, but how sweet it would be to please the Lord with our responses of faith as this centurion did.

Matthew 9 gives us another example of faith: "Some people brought to him a paralytic, lying on a bed. And when Jesus saw their faith, he said to the paralytic, 'Take heart, my son; your sins are forgiven'" (Matthew 9:2). As Jesus was speaking to a crowded room of people, friends of a paralyzed man lowered him from the roof into Jesus' presence. That simple act was the marker of their faith.

Like the centurion, these men did not proclaim their faith in Christ through words; they proclaimed it through action. Matthew 9 also includes the story of the woman with a discharge of blood who touched the fringe of Jesus' robe to make her well. Once again, it was her movement toward Jesus and not any verbal proclamation that revealed the authenticity of her faith in him. This is the example we see repeatedly throughout both the Old and New Testaments. Men and women proclaim their faith, or lack thereof, by their actions. But somehow, over time, our Christian culture has changed the focus of faith from what we do to what we say. Many in the church think we demonstrate faith when we say we believe that Jesus is the only way to God or when we verbally claim to trust him for salvation. We may forcefully tell others that God is sovereign, and we believe him to be in control over our lives. We may stand on our soapbox and proclaim Jesus to be the way, the truth, and the life. But how do we respond to trouble? How do we deal with hardships in life? What good is it if you can verbally defend Christ with the best of believers if your life contradicts your words through anxiety, fear, and worry?

Remember Abraham's example in Genesis 22 when God commanded him to offer Isaac on the altar? As with the centurion in Matthew 8, the friends of the paralytic in Matthew 9, and the woman who touched Jesus' robe, Abraham's faith in God was evidenced by his physical response. He didn't earn God's favor through his works, but he demonstrated his authentic belief by how he responded. James 2:14, 20–22 emphasizes this point:

> What good is it, my brothers, if someone says he has faith but does not have works? Can that faith save him? . . . Do you want to be shown, you foolish person, that faith apart from works is useless? Was not Abraham our father justified by works when he offered up his son Isaac on the altar? You see that faith was active along with his works . . .

When the rubber meets the road, it's not what you say that demonstrates faith in your life. It is what you *do* and how you *respond* in the moment of crisis.

4

Appropriating What You Believe

> But since we belong to the day,
> let us be sober,
> having put on the breastplate of faith and love,
> and for a helmet the hope of salvation.
>
> —1 Thessalonians 5:8

After writing the first draft of this manuscript, I asked a wise friend to read it. Her comment after finishing chapter 3 was this: "You may have convinced readers they have a problem with acting out their faith, but you haven't helped them with a solution." Her words really made me think. We have talked about authentic faith and the value of it in our daily lives. But when the hard times of life are pressing on our hearts, how do we apply what we believe and act faithfully toward God?

Thankfully, the answer is fairly simple. Understanding Hebrews 11:6—that God is the ultimate reality and that confidence in him is fundamental to pleasing him—is the big issue. Once we understand that, our job is simple. We just need to stop and refocus. Have you been dealing with an issue that has sent you into an emotional tailspin? If you are like me, you have allowed your mind to speed through scenarios of how bad the situation might get and what options you have for fixing it on your own. In these situations, the first thing we need to do is *stop*.

Stop

"Stop. Put your pencil down." How many times did we hear that phrase in grade school? It was the standard phrase calling an end to activity for every standardized test I took in school. Now I jokingly use that phrase whenever I want to get someone's attention, especially if that person is involved in an all-consuming activity. When life is crazy, and I'm on an emotional roller coaster powered by fear and worry, I've simply got to *stop*. Cease activity for a moment. Get a grip. Step off the train. Whatever you want to call it, just *stop*! Stop envisioning the worst-case scenarios. Stop thinking through all your options to fix it. You do not have to continue down the path controlled by emotions. After Christ saves us, we are no longer slaves to sin (see Romans 6). *We do not have to obey fear and anxiety as if they were our masters.* Get off the emotional roller coaster! Once you do that, then you can go on to the next step.

Refocus

In Colossians 2 and 3, the apostle Paul gives clear instructions on how to handle sin and struggle in this life. The bottom line of these chapters is that rules won't get you anywhere. Instead, you must hold fast to Jesus Christ. Paul ends this discussion with this summary statement:

> If then you have been raised with Christ, seek the things that are above, where Christ is, seated at the right hand of God. Set your minds on things that are above, not on things that are on earth. For you have died, and your life is hidden with Christ in God. (Colossians 3:1–3)

The instruction is simple—set your heart and mind on Christ and eternity. *Change your perspective and refocus.*

Instead of envisioning the problem at hand, we envision for a moment our God, beautiful in heaven, well aware of our needs, and powerfully able to provide for them. Instead of thinking through our options to fix our problem on our own, we meditate on God's supernatural ability to work out our problems in ways we cannot begin to imagine. Paul reinforces this idea in 2 Corinthians 10:5. He says, "We demolish arguments and every pretension that sets itself up against the knowledge of God, and we take captive every thought to make it obedient to Christ" (NIV). We demolish pretenses (deceptive thought patterns), take captive our thoughts, and set our minds on our spiritual reality.

Let's look again at Hebrews 11. Notice that the Old Testament saints commended in that passage had the same perspective Paul advocates in Colossians 3 and 2 Corinthians 10.

> By faith Noah, being warned by God concerning events as yet unseen, in reverent fear constructed an ark for the saving of his household. By this he condemned the world and became an heir of the righteousness that comes by faith. By faith Abraham obeyed when he was called to go out to a place that he was to receive as an inheritance. And he went out, not knowing where he was going. By faith he went to live in the land of promise, as in a foreign land,

living in tents with Isaac and Jacob, heirs with him of the same promise. For he was looking forward to the city that has foundations, whose designer and builder is God. By faith Sarah herself received power to conceive, even when she was past the age, since she considered him faithful who had promised. . . .

These all died in faith, not having received the things promised, *but having seen them and greeted them from afar, and having acknowledged that they were strangers and exiles on the earth. For people who speak thus make it clear that they are seeking a homeland. If they had been thinking of that land from which they had gone out, they would have had opportunity to return. But as it is, they desire a better country, that is, a heavenly one.* Therefore God is not ashamed to be called their God, for he has prepared for them a city. (Hebrews 11:7–11, 13–16)

The Old Testament saints mentioned in this passage considered themselves strangers on earth and constantly looked toward their heavenly home. They understood their lives were about something much bigger than themselves. It's not that their daily problems were inconsequential. Rather, they had learned to look at their daily struggles from an eternal perspective that provided the context they needed to appropriately deal with those issues. We too must train ourselves to take our thoughts captive and make them submit to what we know to be true about God. We don't ignore the details of this earthly life, but we must always read them in context of our eternal reality.

Abraham and Noah were focused on their eternal home. Eternity with God the Father was their ultimate reality, while this life was only temporary. Years before most of the Word of God was written, these men already understood the concept that James puts forth near the end of the New Testament. He says, "Why, you do not even know what will happen tomorrow. What is your life? You are a mist that appears for a little while and then vanishes" (James 4:14 NIV).

When compared to the extent of eternity, their lives were going to vanish like mere vapors. On this earth, those men saw the eternal end result from afar, but they still found all-enduring hope in the wealth of God's promises for the future. They demonstrated for us godly perspective by filtering the issues of life through faith in God's promises.

Once we get off the emotional roller coaster that's directing our responses and refocus our spiritual lens to a God honoring perspective, then we start anew in light of eternity. There is no rocket science here. This is not "Twenty Ways to Make God Pleased with You" or "Five Steps to Faith-filled Living." It's not that complicated.

Practice

Let me elaborate on an example I mentioned earlier of how God corrected my vision, enabling me to refocus on him as I drove home after a trying day at work. This was not a particularly profound trial, but it seemed large to me at the time. I was very dissatisfied with my job. I wondered why I was there, if I should quit, and if I had made a series of colossal mistakes in the choices that had led me to that job. In that moment, I remembered how my husband had encouraged me through a similar struggle a few weeks before by getting my attention and simply asking me exactly what I believed about God. So I sat in my car at the stoplight, ended the destructive mental path I was following, and asked myself, "Now what is it that I believe about God?" My first thought was that this life is just a vapor. God is eternal, but this job situation was not. Compared to the scope of God's eternity, this job struggle was a mist in the morning that would soon evaporate. I moved on to meditate on other attributes of God and thought about his power over all circumstances as outlined in Colossians 1:17: "He is before all things, and in him all things hold together." I then finished up with a review of his plan to work all things for my good and his glory (see Romans 8:28).

Of course, I didn't think through those things then as coherently as I've presented them here. In reality, that thought process was a stream of consciousness during the time I sat at the stoplight. That quick reflection served as my spiritual lens adjustment, putting God's eternal purposes back as the center of my attention. My current job struggle was definitely still in my line of vision, but it no longer demanded my focus or consumed my energy.

So how do we appropriate what we believe about God? The bottom line is that, with God's help, we must stop in the middle of our struggles and force our line of vision back on the eternal perspective. When my two dogs get excited, usually due to the presence of a cat or squirrel in their vicinity, they do not respond to anything I say. Often, the only option I have for getting their attention is to grab their little chins and turn their faces back toward me. Only then do they get the message I am trying to communicate. Similarly, when I get excited and consumed by the emotional roller coaster of life, I need to figuratively grab my chin and turn my head back toward God. I need an eternal perspective that sees God as the ultimate reality. All else will pale in comparison when viewed against the backdrop of his eternal purposes.

What things in your life seem out of control? What is the focus of your anxieties? Is it getting a husband, paying bills, or losing weight? Are your kids out of control? Is your marriage failing? Do you have health problems or broken friendships? Once you've named the issues over which you are struggling, stop the emotional roller coaster and review what you believe about God. If you aren't sure what you believe about him, his character, and his purposes, the rest of this book should be a help to you. You need to both identify the truth of God's character and take practical steps to speak that truth to your heart. This may mean unplugging the computer or phone, turning off the TV, and shutting yourself off until you have memorized some Scripture on the trustworthiness of God. Ask God to show you practical ways for you to refocus on his character and purposes.

For Further Study

Women of faith in the Bible:

Ruth: Book of Ruth

Abigail: 1 Samuel 25

Esther: Book of Esther

Unnamed women: Matthew 9:20–22; Luke 7:36, 50

Mary of Bethany and Martha: Luke 10:38–41; John 11; John 12:1–8

Lydia: Acts 16:11–15

Phoebe: Romans 16:1–2

5

Practical Theology Indeed!

If we are faithless, he remains faithful—
for he cannot deny himself.

—2 Timothy 2:13

We have talked about what faith looked like in the lives of both Old and New Testament believers and have thought through the process of applying it to our own lives. I have a good deal of personal experience putting this into practice. As I mentioned before, in a two-year time period, my husband, Andy, and I endured a series of trials that both tested and strengthened our faith. Andy was unemployed for nearly a year. Six weeks after starting his new job, he was diagnosed with a heart condition that required immediate open-heart surgery. A few months after his surgery, Andy returned to work, and I became pregnant. We miscarried a few weeks later and entered a season of desiring a child while having problems conceiving. I remember recounting this to a friend at the time. Her response was, "Wow, everything bad happens to you." That is not a very helpful statement to make to someone who is hurting. And yet, as I looked at my life, I could see the good hand of God constantly at work. Each trial taught us beautiful things about God—things that are so precious to know about him that it was worth the earthly pain we endured to learn it.

Faith and Praise

During our struggles, we learned to wholeheartedly praise God in the good times and the bad. Most importantly, we learned that God is every bit as good in the hard times as he is in the times of plenty. In fact, often he seems more beautiful and sustaining during the trials, perhaps because he has forcefully removed from our line of vision the things that obscure our view of him. In our lives, Habakuk 3:17–19 became less like a goal and more like reality:

> Though the fig tree should not blossom,
>> nor fruit be on the vines,
> the produce of the olive fail
>> and the fields yield no food,
> the flock be cut off from the fold
>> and there be no herd in the stalls,
> yet I will rejoice in the LORD;
>> I will take joy in the God of my salvation.
> GOD, the Lord, is my strength;
>> he makes my feet like the deer's;
>> he makes me tread on my high places.

Note that there is no praise of man in that passage. It's not that when the going got tough, the tough got going. The point is that when the going got tough and the weak were curled up in bed in the fetal position, Christ surrounded them with his hands, his feet, and his body, and held them tightly to his bosom so that they could see only his face. For Andy and me, that was when the trials became beautiful.

As time passed, Andy and I became more and more convinced of God's uncanny ability to turn horrible circumstances into precious treasures. In particular, through our time of unemployment, serious illness, miscarriage, and infertility, our brothers and sisters in Christ ministered to us in ways that revealed precious glimpses of God's character and splendor. God made it clear to us that he is trustworthy, he is good, and he truly works all things "for the good of those who love him [and] have been called according to his purpose" (Romans 8:28 NIV). I look back at the times that I doubted God's goodness, and I laugh at my ignorance. Our trials, though painful for Andy and me, have brought about the most wonderful blessings in our lives. Like Moses in Exodus 33, through trials we caught a glimpse of God's glory, and it is the most beautiful thing we have ever seen.

So let's bring this section full circle. Theology, at its most basic sense, is simply the study of God. Proper theology is not complex, but it is fundamentally important for all believers, because knowing our God and understanding his character are essential tools that enable us to exercise wisdom in our daily lives. As we study who God is and what he does, we are equipped to deal with the big and small issues of life. Knowing God and acting in faith in light of those beliefs is key to a life that is pleasing to God. *Know him, and then act like you know him.* That is faith.

Part *two*

Who Is Our God?

"But let him who boasts boast in this:
that he understands and knows me,
that I am the LORD, who practices steadfast love,
justice, and righteousness in the earth.
For in these things I delight, declares the LORD"

—Jeremiah 9:24

In the first chapter of this book, we established the fundamental value of the study of theology in a believer's life. Next, we focused on Hebrews 11:6, where God states a major tenet of his plan for simplifying our sin-complicated lives—"without faith it is impossible to please him." After telling us that it is impossible to please God apart from faith, the author of Hebrews becomes even more specific, emphasizing that we must specifically believe that God exists and that he rewards those who diligently seek him. In essence, the author of Hebrews is telling us that the heart of faith is a *right view of God*.

What do I mean by a "right view of God"? Well, many of us come to God with unbiblical notions of who he is and what he does. We've let our culture and upbringing, rather than the Bible itself, determine the character traits we attribute to God. Is your God vindictive or permissive? Is he "hands off" or "hands on"? Is he personal or unapproachable? For many of us, the way we answer those questions has nothing to do with what the Bible teaches about God and everything to do with our culture and upbringing. Authentic faith in God is based on an understanding of the *truth* of God's character that comes from Scripture alone, along with confidence in the trustworthiness of that truth when applied practically to our daily lives.

This naturally leads to the next question, which is of utmost importance—what exactly does the Bible teach us about the character and attributes of our God?

6

God Is Our Father

"I will be a Father to you, and you shall be
sons and daughters to me," says the Lord Almighty.
—2 Corinthians 6:18

Let's start our examination of God with a look at the Father.
Through faith in Christ, we have become children of Almighty
God. Christ's instructions on prayer in the Gospels reflect this
reality. Jesus instructs the disciples to call his Father "Our Father"
(Matthew 6:9). This is a concept worthy of serious meditation—the
Father of Jesus Christ is now our Father too!

Adopted by God

We have been adopted into God's family and our position as his children is forever secure.

Often the best way to understand a theological concept is simply to read in context the Scripture that describes it. In Romans 8, the apostle Paul explains in detail our relationship to God the Father:

> There is therefore now no condemnation for those who are in Christ Jesus. For the law of the Spirit of life has set you free in Christ Jesus from the law of sin and death.... So then, brothers, we are debtors, not to the flesh, to live according to the flesh. For if you live according to the flesh you will die, but if by the Spirit you put to death the deeds of the body, you will live. For all who are led by the Spirit of God are sons of God. For you did not receive the spirit of slavery to fall back into fear, but you have received the Spirit of adoption as sons, by whom we cry, "Abba! Father!" The Spirit himself bears witness with our spirit that we are children of God, and if children, then heirs—heirs of God and fellow heirs with Christ, provided we suffer with him in order that we may also be glorified with him.
>
> For I consider that the sufferings of this present time are not worth comparing with the glory that is to be revealed to us. For the creation waits with eager longing for the revealing of the sons of God.... And not only the creation, but we ourselves, who have the firstfruits of the Spirit, groan inwardly as we wait eagerly for adoption as sons, the redemption of our bodies. (Romans 8:1–2, 12–19, 23)

Before salvation, we were enemies of God. However, according to John 1:12, God has given "the right to become children of God" to all those who believe in Christ. In Romans 8, Paul says we are adopted into God's family. Did you notice that Paul here contrasts our former position as a *slave* to sin and fear to our new position as a *child* of God and *fellow heir* with Christ? We're not just adopted into God's family as some token charity case. We are adopted into his family with the highest of honors—given the title of fellow-heir with Jesus Christ. To me, being called an heir of God on a par with God the Son sounds almost sacrilegious. Yet, that is exactly the position we hold as adopted children of God the Father. This is indeed the most awesome turnaround in fortunes!

In Galatians, Paul again contrasts our former position as slaves to our current position as sons of God and heirs of his fortune:

> In Christ Jesus you are all sons of God, through faith. For as many of you as were baptized into Christ have put on Christ. . . . But when the fullness of time had come, God sent forth his Son, born of woman, born under the law, to redeem those who were under the law, so that *we might receive adoption as sons*. And because you are sons, God has sent the Spirit of his Son into our hearts, crying, "Abba! Father!" So you are no longer a slave, but a son, and if a son, then an heir through God. (Galatians 3:26–27; 4:4–7)

In these passages, the apostle Paul makes clear the full benefits of our adoption into God's family. In Romans 8 and Galatians 3–4, he emphasizes our high position in God's household. In the next passage, Paul emphasizes that God's adoption of each of us was well thought out before time began. God wanted *you* in his family before he created the world!

> He chose us in him before the foundation of the world, that we should be holy and blameless before him. In love he predestined us for adoption as sons through Jesus Christ, according to the purpose of his will, to the praise of his glorious grace, with which he has blessed us in the Beloved. (Ephesians 1:4–6)

There is much more to explore in these passages than we will do in this book. For now, let's meditate upon the major points we've covered: in Christ, we are adopted into God's family; we are established in the incredible position of fellow heir with Christ; and this plan was put in motion by God before time began.

In addition to these great truths, our position as God's children is secure. In fact, the Bible calls the Holy Spirit the deposit and guarantee that God will fulfill his commitment to us (see 2 Corinthians 1:21–22). Later, we'll explore more of the names of the Holy Spirit and his role in this process, but for right now rest in the *security* of our position as children of God with all the benefits that come with being a child of the Most High. Lay aside your agenda for a moment. Stop striving to relieve yourself of the burdens that plague you. Rest, dear sister. Rest in the secure arms of your heavenly Father, who set your story in motion before time began.

7

Our Father Is Sovereign, Compassionate, and Wise

"Are not two sparrows sold for a penny?
And not one of them will fall to the ground
apart from your Father."

—Matthew 10:29

o understand the full benefits of being adopted into God's family, we need to study the attributes of our Father. What is it that makes God, well, God? What makes him holy, i.e., completely unique and set apart from all others? The thing that sets God apart is his sovereignty. He is completely self-sustaining and self-governing. He answers to no one while

> **sov·er·eign**
>
> n. One that exercises supreme, permanent authority ... adj. Self-governing; independent.*
>
> * The American Heritage Dictionary of the English Language, 4th ed.

all answer to him. Consider what the following Scriptures reveal about our Father. Then spend a few moments contemplating what it means for you that your Father is the supreme authority over all circumstances, involving all people, for all time.

> Whatever the LORD pleases, he does,
>> in heaven and on earth,
>> in the seas and all deeps. (Psalm 135:6)

> ". . . remember the former things of old;
> for I am God, and there is no other;
>> I am God, and there is none like me,
> declaring the end from the beginning
>> and from ancient times things not yet done,
> saying, 'My counsel shall stand,
>> and I will accomplish all my purpose,'
> calling a bird of prey from the east,
>> the man of my counsel from a far country.
> I have spoken, and I will bring it to pass;
>> I have purposed, and I will do it." (Isaiah 46:9–11)

> "All the inhabitants of the earth are accounted as nothing,
>> and he does according to his will among the host of heaven
>> and among the inhabitants of the earth;
> and none can stay his hand
>> or say to him, 'What have you done?'" (Daniel 4:35)

Sovereign

According to these passages, God knows the end from the beginning and his purposes always stand. He does whatever pleases himself, and no one can hold back his hand from accomplishing what he intends to do. In the next passages, notice the details revealed about God's purposes and plans from before time began.

> He chose us in him before the foundation of the world, that we should be holy and blameless before him. . . . Making known to us the mystery of his will, according to his purpose, which he set forth in Christ as a plan for the fullness of time, to unite all things in him, things in heaven and things on earth. In him we have obtained an inheritance, having been predestined according to the purpose of him who works all things according to the counsel of his will. (Ephesians 1:4, 9–11)

> But we ought always to give thanks to God for you, brothers beloved by the Lord, because God chose you as the firstfruits to be saved, through sanctification by the Spirit and belief in the truth. (2 Thessalonians 2:13)

> [He] saved us and called us to a holy calling, not because of our works but because of his own purpose and grace, which he gave us in Christ Jesus before the ages began. (2 Timothy 1:9)

God has planned our salvation since before the earth was created, and despite man's wickedness, God has never lost control. I find daily comfort in the knowledge that God chose me for himself before he had even created the world and that he perfectly works out his plan according to his will. Our Father is truly a rock in the midst of the raging storms of life. We can cling to his unchanging purposes and uncompromising nature to sustain us when we are battered by the seeming chaos of life.

The next passages give us even more evidence of our Father's power. Our Father is sovereign over the good actions of men, the wicked actions of men, and so-called accidental events. What a comforting doctrine!

For we are his workmanship, created in Christ Jesus for good works, which God prepared beforehand, that we should walk in them. (Ephesians 2:10)

> "This Jesus, delivered up according to the definite plan and foreknowledge of God, you crucified and killed by the hands of lawless men." (Acts 2:23)

> The LORD has made everything for its purpose,
>> even the wicked for the day of trouble.
>> (Proverbs 16:4)

> The lot is cast into the lap,
>> but its every decision is from the LORD.
>> (Proverbs 16:33)

God has had a plan for us since before time began, a plan that included sending his Son to die for our sins. Despite the evil and hard circumstances we see and experience in this world, we can trust that our Father hasn't lost control and that he, in fact, retains his sovereign rights over the fallout. Consider Joseph in Genesis 37–50. He was sold into slavery by his brothers, accused of rape by the lustful wife of his boss, and unfairly thrown into prison. Yet, in the end, Joseph was able to say to his brothers that though they "meant evil against [him] . . . God meant it for good, to bring it about that many people should be kept alive" (Genesis 50:20). To me, this is the ultimate, miraculous characteristic of our Father. *He alone has the amazing ability to turn the worst of circumstances into something beautiful and precious for his name's sake.* As Paul states in Romans 8:28, "We know that for those who love God all things work together for good, for those who are called according to his purpose."

Examine yourself for a moment. What does confidence in God's sovereignty look like in your life? Do you demonstrate trust in God's plan and purposes or become fearful and anxious when circumstances spiral out of your control? Do your reactions to the hard things in life reflect confidence in God's promise to work even the bad situations for your good? Or do you become frustrated and depressed when circumstances don't turn out as you think they should? Is your first reaction to trials to think fast and do something or to rest and wait patiently for God's hand to work? As we've said before, many of us *say* we believe "God is in control," but our daily responses to life's issues reflect a different belief altogether. Once again, the key to overcoming with joy in this life is to align our responses to hard things with what we know to be true about our heavenly Father.

Compassionate and Wise

"As a father shows compassion to his children, so the LORD shows compassion to those who fear him" (Psalm 103:13).

Our Father in heaven is sovereign, but sovereignty alone is not necessarily a comforting trait. History is full of powerful rulers who were despised by their subjects. Thankfully, not only is our Father sovereign, but he is also good. In particular, our Father has great compassion for his children. I was fortunate to grow up with a father who showed his children compassion, protection, and provision. However, many women have not had that privilege. Often, by default, we attribute to God the characteristics of our fallen, earthly fathers. Many women have no confidence that God is going to provide for them because their own dads did not provide for them. The challenge before us is to strip away our views of God that come from our earthly fathers or authority figures and replace them with the right view of God presented in Scripture.

> In the fear of the LORD one has strong confidence,
>   and his children will have a refuge. (Proverbs 14:26)

73

"But if God so clothes the grass of the field, which today is alive and tomorrow is thrown into the oven, will he not much more clothe you, O you of little faith? Therefore do not be anxious, saying, 'What shall we eat?' or 'What shall we drink?' or 'What shall we wear?' For the Gentiles seek after all these things, and your heavenly Father knows that you need them all." (Matthew 6:30–32)

Our Father is both sovereign and compassionate. While these are valuable attributes, there is a third aspect of his character that is of fundamental importance. Our Father is also *wise*. If God's judgments weren't wise, right, and trustworthy, we'd be sunk. A strong, loving god wouldn't be that great if he didn't know what he were doing! Romans 16:27 says, "To the only wise God be glory forevermore through Jesus Christ!" Our Father is strong, compassionate, and wise. His judgments are trustworthy because they are always *right*. God doesn't make wrong choices. He sees the end from the beginning and leads us accordingly.

What is even more beautiful is that our wise, compassionate, and sovereign Father invites us, through Christ, to communicate with him. Our Father wants a relationship with us.

In [Christ] we have boldness and access with confidence through our faith in him. (Ephesians 3:12)

Let us then with confidence draw near to the throne of grace, that we may receive mercy and find grace to help in time of need. (Hebrews 4:16)

Let's examine ourselves again against this teaching. Do you approach your sovereign, compassionate, and wise Father with confidence, believing that he *wants* a relationship with you? Or do you see God as standoffish like the distant father with whom you grew up? Do you find yourself acting as if God is out to get you, or do you interpret hard circumstances in light of his promised compassion and provision for you, his child? Do you feel you must control your circumstances because you don't trust God to make wise choices that are in your best interest? Or do you let confidence in his wisdom govern your responses?

Our wise and sovereign God has adopted us into his family and invites us to come into his presence and partake of his grace and goodness. Furthermore, he has compassion and pity for his children, and all his actions toward his children are consistent with his compassion, love, and wisdom. These are important facts to remember as we explore the next implication of being a child of God.

For Further Study

Packer, J. I. *Knowing God.* Downers Grove, IL: InterVarsity, 1973; 1993.

8

Our Father Disciplines Us

My son, do not despise the LORD's discipline
or be weary of his reproof,
for the LORD reproves him whom he loves,
as a father the son in whom he delights.

—Proverbs 3:11–12

ne of the great benefits of being adopted into God's family is that we receive his discipline. Often we do not think of that as a benefit, but that's because many of us have warped views of discipline and its purpose. What is discipline? According to *The American Heritage Dictionary* discipline is "training expected to produce a specific character or pattern of behavior, especially training that produces moral or mental improvement."[1] The problem is that the vast majority of us have experienced a warped form of discipline from those in authority over us. Many times, authority figures

dis·ci·pline

n. Training expected to produce a specific character or pattern of behavior, especially training that produces moral or mental improvement.

meted out punishment when they should have exercised discipline. In light of these practical experiences, we tend to confuse the two theologically as well.

According to Romans 8:1, Christ bore the full weight of our punishment for sin on the cross, and we are no longer condemned for our sin. This is the very good news of the gospel. Then in Romans 8:29, we learn that God's plan before time began is to transform us into the likeness of his Son. This is why we need discipline, i.e., training in righteousness.

> There is therefore now no condemnation for those who are in Christ Jesus. For the law of the Spirit of life has set you free in Christ Jesus from the law of sin and death. . . . For those whom he foreknew he also predestined to be conformed to the image of his Son, in order that he might be the firstborn among many brothers. (Romans 8:1–2, 29)

Instead of punishing us for our sins, God the Father poured out his full wrath for our sins on Jesus at the cross. Now, God disciplines us to mold us into the image of his Son, purifying us by rooting out the sin in our lives and replacing it with behavior and attitudes that reflect Christ.

"Those whom I love, I reprove and discipline so be zealous and repent" (Revelation 3:19). However, instead of being earnest and repenting, many of us chafe at God's discipline. We despise God's training to produce Christlike behavior in us. We would rather be naked orphans running about on the street stealing food than God's adopted children who accept his rebuke and correction. In contrast to the purpose for punishment (which is payment of the penalty for our sin), the purpose of discipline is transformation—for us to grow less and less like ourselves and more and more like Christ. Granted, discipline is often hard. In Hebrews 12:6, the word that is translated "punish" literally means "to scourge." The use of this word in the Greek doesn't reflect penalty for sin. Instead, it refers to harsh discipline used to change behavior rather than punish it. It's a strong word that reminds us that, at times, God's hand of discipline can be severe. Though his methods are not always pleasant, the result most certainly is. We are becoming less like ourselves and more like Jesus Christ. Such a result makes God's rebuke and correction well worth it. It is by God's *mercy* and *grace* that he doesn't leave us as he finds us!

And have you forgotten the exhortation that addresses you as sons?

> "My son, do not regard lightly the discipline of the Lord,
>   nor be weary when reproved by him.
> For the Lord disciplines the one he loves,
>   and chastises every son whom he receives."

It is for discipline that you have to endure. God is treating you as sons. For what son is there whom his father does not discipline? If you are left without discipline, in which all have participated, then you are illegitimate children and not sons. Besides this, we have had earthly fathers who disciplined us and we respected them. Shall we not much more be subject to the Father of spirits and live? For they disciplined us for a short time as it seemed best to them, but he disciplines us for our good, that we may share his holiness. For the moment all discipline seems painful rather than pleasant, but later it yields the peaceful fruit of righteousness to those who have been trained by it. (Hebrews 12:5–11)

Love in Discipline

We cannot overemphasize that being disciplined by our heavenly Father is a good thing. Remember that the end result of this process is our transformation into the beautiful, radiant bride of Christ. Do you believe that becoming people who respond more like Christ and less like we were when God found us is a good thing? Do you think that learning to respond to circumstances like Christ responded is good for you? While I have never enjoyed God's discipline, I have been greatly blessed by the results. It is God's goodness toward us that he doesn't allow us to continue in sin but instead roots sin out of our lives and replaces it with attitudes and actions that reflect those of Christ. It's only through being conformed to the image of Christ that we can begin to experience the joy and peace for which so many of us long.

As we conclude our discussion on the character of our Father, note that Romans 8 tells us that we have experienced the *firstfruits* of our adoption. In other words, we have experienced on earth only the very beginning of the blessings of this adoption. The greatest harvest will come in eternity. We eagerly look to the day that our bodies are redeemed and we are fully liberated from the troubles of this life.

> For you did not receive the spirit of slavery to fall back into fear, but you have received the Spirit of adoption as sons, by whom we cry, "Abba! Father!" (Romans 8:15)

The culmination of our adoption into God's family will occur when we are delivered into heaven, completely redeemed and rescued from *all* that plagues us by our depravity. We are children of God who have barely begun to taste the full beauty of our inheritance.

When you couple God's sovereignty and wisdom with his compassion for his children, it's an unbeatable deal. Your Father in heaven is in control, loves you, and knows what he's doing. No matter what kind of father you knew as a child, your eternal

Father does what he says. No man can change God's purposes, and his fundamental purpose in your life is to transform you into the image of Christ for his glory. That is a very good thing! Our heavenly Father is not just generally aware of our needs. Instead, he is intimately acquainted with all the details of our lives and has a purpose and plan for them all. He is faithful to his Word, so curl up in his arms tonight and sleep in perfect peace.

> Father of the fatherless and protector of widows
>   is God in his holy habitation. (Psalm 68:5)

Now on to our fellow heir.

9

God Is Our Savior, Example, and Bridegroom

He is the image of the invisible God,
the firstborn of all creation.

—Colossians 1:15

reviously we discussed that theology, the study of the character and attributes of God, is vital if we want to be wise stewards of the life God has prepared for us. We need to know what we believe about God and then act consistently with those beliefs when confronted with the daily issues of life.

We have studied our sovereign Father and meditated on the bene-fits of our adoption into his family. Now we move our focus to God the Son, Jesus Christ. Matthew 11:27 states that "no one knows the Father except the Son and anyone to whom the Son chooses to reveal him." We cannot separate knowledge of God the Father from a relationship with God the Son. Scripture says that Jesus Christ "is the radiance of the glory of God and the exact imprint of his nature, and he upholds the universe by the word of his power" (Hebrews 1:3). Therefore, if we want to know God, *we must know Jesus Christ.* As we study him, the knowledge of Christ's character and work will open our eyes to greater depths of God's character. Core to understanding Christ is the fact that Jesus is both God and man. According to John 1, Jesus is the Word who was God, was with God, and came to us in the flesh. This means that in the single person of Jesus is both a human and divine nature. He is not merely a man who had God in him, nor is he simply a man who exhibited godlike characteristics. He is God, second person of the Trinity.

> In the beginning was the Word, and the Word was with God, and the Word was God.... And the Word became flesh and dwelt among us, and we have seen his glory, glory as of the only Son from the Father, full of grace and truth. (John 1:1, 14)

> I and the Father are one. (John 10:30)

The Identity of Jesus

Jesus was and is fully God and fully man. This is a doctrine that we as finite humans are incapable of completely understanding. Jesus as God was worshiped (see Matthew 14:33). Jesus as man worshiped the Father (see John 17). Jesus as God was sinless (see 1 Peter 2:22). Jesus as man was tempted to sin (see Matthew 4:1). Jesus as God knows all things (see John 21:17). Jesus as man grew in wisdom (see Luke 2:52). Jesus as God gives eternal life (see John 10:28). Jesus as man died (see Romans 5:8).

Our infinite God came to earth as a finite human being! Have you wrestled with this doctrine and meditated upon its ramifications? If Jesus was just a good man, then his death on the cross, while commendable and selfless, is not worthy of great notice because he would not have been the first man to die for another. But if Jesus is *God*, then his death on the cross means something else entirely! It is profoundly humbling to think that the God of the Universe lowered himself to die naked on a cross, feeling both the acute physical pain of a human and the excruciating spiritual pain of Holy God as the weight of our sin lay on his shoulders. This reminds me of one of my favorite hymns by Charles Wesley, "Amazing Love." I'm always struck by the power of Wesley's question, "Amazing love, how can it be that Thou, my God, shouldst die for me?" I've noticed lately some Christian artists changing the final phrase to "Thou, my King" rather than "Thou, my God." Perhaps there are no ulterior motives meant by that change, but I find it extremely disturbing. The power of the crucifixion is that our *God*, Sovereign Lord of the Universe, humbled himself to die in our place.

I've rarely heard a nonbeliever argue that Christ never lived. People don't seem to have a problem accepting that Jesus was a real man. The issue core to belief has always been whether Christ is actually God. During his earthly life, Christ's humanity was readily evident to those who knew him. It was always his deity that the religious establishment could not or would not grasp. In John 1, we are told that Jesus was God, but the darkness could not understand it. Jesus repeatedly did miraculous signs and wonders, even raising the dead back to life. Yet, his own people in their blindness denied his deity and killed him.

He was in the world, and the world was made through him, yet the world did not know him. He came to his own, and his own people did not receive him. (John 1:10–11)

Coming to his hometown he taught them in their synagogue, so that they were astonished, and said, "Where did this man get this wisdom and these mighty works? Is not this the carpenter's son? Is not his mother called Mary? And are not his brothers James and Joseph and Simon and Judas? And are not all his sisters with us? Where then did this man get all these things?" And they took offense at him. But Jesus said to them, "A prophet is not without honor except in his hometown and in his own household." And he did not do many mighty works there, because of their unbelief. (Matthew 13:54–58)

Kenosis

The paradox between Christ's deity and his humanity is encapsulated in the theological concept known as *kenosis*. This doctrine is based on Paul's words concerning Christ in Philippians 2.

Do nothing from selfishness or empty conceit, but with humility of mind regard one another as more important than yourselves; do not merely look out for your own personal interests, but also for the interests of others. Have this attitude in yourselves which was also in Christ Jesus, who, although He existed in the form of God, did not regard equality with God a thing to be grasped, but emptied Himself, taking the form of a bond-servant, and being made in the likeness of men. Being found in appearance as a man, He humbled Himself by becoming obedient to the point of death, even death on a cross. (Philippians 2:3–8 NASB)

The word translated "emptied" in verse 7 is the Greek word *kenoō*, which means to empty, void, or deprive.[1] Of what was Christ emptying himself? Though he was fully God with all the powers and rights that sovereignty provided him, he willingly deprived himself of those rights.

The NIV and ESV translate *kenoō* as "made himself nothing." The KJV says "made Himself of no reputation." Rather than grasping all of his rights and power as sovereign God, Christ made himself *nothing* for our sake. It is not that he thought badly of himself. The point is that he did not think of himself *at all*. He opened his hands and willingly let go of his rights, forgetting about himself completely. He allowed himself to be maligned, spat upon, treated as a bastard, liar, and traitor, and ultimately allowed himself to be murdered.

Furthermore, Philippians 2 commands us to be ruled by the kind of thinking that ruled Christ. We are called to willingly give up our rights and welcome the sacrifices that accompany being a servant to others. We are not called to think badly of ourselves. People who think badly of themselves are as self-centered as those who think highly of themselves. *Instead, we are called not to think of ourselves at all.* As our grasp on our perceived rights weakens, our needs fade into the background, and we become little images of Christ—consumed with the needs of others to the forgetfulness of our own.

This is so counter to our culture. It is not natural to humbly consider others as more important than ourselves. Yet, this is exactly what our God did by coming to earth and dying for us. Honestly, whose life is more important—yours or God's? Who most deserves to live? Who will most influence others positively? Who is the most beautiful? Who is the most just? In an honest comparison, we *know* that we don't deserve to live if our living costs the life of God. However, defying all natural wisdom, Jesus considered our lives above his own. He considered God's plan for salvation more important than his rights; he emptied himself and died in our place. Now he calls us to adopt his humble attitude.

How would emptying yourself of your rights be revealed in your life? In my life, I constantly struggle with my desire to defend my rights and guard my reputation. When I perceive that I have been treated unjustly, I protect my interests in a wave of righteous indignation, unaware of the unrighteousness of my attempts to defend myself. Christ tells us to turn the other cheek and to forgive excessively when we are wronged. Ephesians 4:32 reminds us that we forgive others not because they deserve it, but because God through Christ has forgiven us of so much more. As we become more like Christ, we let go of our reputation. We are no longer consumed with protecting our rights. We forgive the one who has hurt us, but only through the power of Christ's example. Our understanding of and appreciation for Christ is our *only* hope of getting this right in our lives day in and day out.

Our Example

Let's deal honestly with a fact that you and I both know well—living humbly in an unjust world is tough, especially for women. You don't have to read far in a history book or even today's newspaper to see that women have been and are still being exploited and abused throughout the world. This book is not intended as a biblical treatise on women's issues. Suffice it to say for our purposes that women were created in the image of God, Satan has worked hard to destroy the dignity of that image in women, and we should fight for justice against such abuse, as the Bible demands. But the answer to such abuse is not that we abandon God's instructions to women to be like Jesus. As we grapple with humble submission, we can take comfort and direction from Jesus' own example. He models it most clearly for us in the garden in Luke 22 as he wrestles in prayer with the Father over his imminent death on the cross. Jesus doesn't put on false cheer. He is honest about his pain and struggle, sweating drops of blood in his agony. This picture sustains me when I wrestle with the Father over submission in hard times, painfully, tearfully, earnestly presenting my cause, and then submitting to his plan and purposes for me—"not my will but yours. Not my reputation, but yours. Not my agenda, but yours. Not my rights, but yours."

Justification

What did Jesus accomplish for us through his life and death? As the Son of God, who emptied himself of his rights as God, Jesus endured the Father's wrath in our place. Paul teaches in 2 Corinthians 5:21 that "for our sake he made him to be sin who knew no sin, so that in him we might become the righteousness of God."

At the fall of man in the garden of Eden, all of Adam's descendants inherited his sinful nature. Our spiritual DNA is corrupt and depraved. The result is spiritual death, which leads to physical death (see Romans 5:12). The Bible says that we were dead in our sinful state and without hope of reviving ourselves. We were condemned by our sin before our Judge, the righteous and holy God, who cannot tolerate sin.

> And you were dead in the trespasses and sins in which you once walked, following the course of this world, following the prince of the power of the air, the spirit that is now at work in the sons of disobedience—among whom we all once lived in the passions of our flesh, carrying out the desires of the body and the mind, and were by nature children of wrath, like the rest of mankind. But God, being rich in mercy, because of the great love with which he loved us, even when we were dead in our trespasses, made us alive together with Christ. (Ephesians 2:1–5)

"But God." These are surely the two most beautiful words in all of Scripture. Paul says that though we were dead in our sins, God in his mercy made us alive with Christ.

Because of our inability to keep God's righteous law, we deserved death and judgment. In our place, God sent his Son to die on the cross as our substitute. At his death, God placed all our sins on Christ's shoulders, and in exchange he placed Christ's righteousness on our account. In Isaiah 61:10, the prophet Isaiah paints the beautiful word picture of God clothing us in the "garments of salvation" and a "robe of righteousness." Consider the contrast: Jesus Christ— sinless, compassionate, and perfect Son of God—was literally stripped of his garments and hung naked on the cross, while God clothed us—naked, blind, and rotting in our sin—with Christ's robe of righteousness.

> For Christ also suffered once for sins, the righteous for the unrighteous, that he might bring us to God, being put to death in the flesh but made alive in the spirit. (1 Peter 3:18)

> v. **justify** (Gk. dikaioō)
> 1. to render righteous or such he ought to be
> 2. to show, exhibit, evince, one to be righteous, such as he is and wishes himself to be considered
> 3. to declare, pronounce, one to be just, righteous, or such as he ought to be

This is *justification*. Though our best works were like dirty menstrual rags in God's eyes (see Isaiah 64:6), he declared us righteous by switching our sins to Christ's shoulders and Christ's righteousness to our account. We were alienated from God, but now we have been declared righteous through Christ's blood and can confidently approach the throne of God. We are now reconciled to God and have free access to his presence.

> Therefore, brothers, since we have confidence to enter the holy places by the blood of Jesus, by the new and living way that he opened for us through the curtain, that is, through his flesh…let us draw near with a true heart in full assurance of faith, with our hearts sprinkled clean from an evil conscience and our bodies washed with pure water. (Hebrews 10:19–20, 22)

Glorification

Through his death on the cross, Christ has cleared the way for our reconciliation to God. Romans 8:29–30 (NIV) sets up the progression of our spiritual lives for us: "For those God foreknew he also predestined to be conformed to the likeness of his Son, that he might be the firstborn among many brothers. And those he predestined, he also called; those he called, he also justified; those he justified, he also glorified."

God knew us before time began (foreknowledge). He predetermined to conform us to Christ's image. He called us to himself, he justified us by switching our sin to Christ and Christ's righteousness to us, and the final stop in that progression is known as *glorification.* The Greek word means "to make glorious" or "to clothe with splendor." To understand the spiritual concept of glorification, compare our state before salvation in which "all have sinned and fall short of the glory of God" (Romans 3:23) to the state of those who know Christ in 2 Corinthians 3:18: "But we all, with unveiled face,

> v. **glorify** (Gr. doxazō)
>
> To praise, extol, magnify, celebrate; to honor, do honor to, hold in honor; to make glorious, adorn with luster, clothe with splendor; to impart glory to something, render it excellent; to make renowned, render illustrious; to cause the dignity and worth of some person or thing to become manifest and acknowledged.

beholding as in a mirror the glory of the Lord, are being transformed into the same image from glory to glory, just as from the Lord, the Spirit" (NASB).

God doesn't just declare us righteous and leave us to our own evil desires for the rest of our lives. God *transforms* us into children who truly reflect his glory. The process of transforming us into his image is called sanctification, which we'll explore in a later chapter. The end result of all this is our glorification. When Scripture talks about this doctrine, it often uses marriage to illustrate the concept.

> Husbands, love your wives, just as Christ also loved the church and gave Himself for her, that He might sanctify and cleanse her with the washing of water by the word, that He might present her to Himself a glorious church, not having spot or wrinkle or any such thing, but that she should be holy and without blemish. (Ephesians 5:25–27 NKJV)

You can easily identify a marriage where the husband reflects Christ in this matter. A well-loved wife married to a Christ-like husband grows in her beauty, inside and out, so that she is more glorious after fifteen years of marriage than she was on her wedding day. This growth in inner and outer beauty defines the relationship between the perfect Bridegroom, Jesus Christ, and his imperfect bride, the church. We started out as slaves to sin. Then Christ redeemed us, buying us out of slavery and setting us up in his household. However, he didn't just make us slaves to a new and kind master. Instead, he elevates us to the honored and cherished position of his wife.

> "In that day," declares the LORD, "you will call me 'my husband'; you will no longer call me 'my master.'... I will betroth you to me forever; I will betroth you in righteousness and justice, in love and compassion. I will betroth you in faithfulness, and you will acknowledge the LORD." (Hosea 2:16, 19–20 NIV)

The culmination of this glorification will be at the marriage supper of the Lamb. This is our future hope as the bride of Christ, described for us at the end of Revelation.

> "Let us be glad and rejoice and give Him glory, for the marriage of the Lamb has come, and His wife has made herself ready." And to her it was granted to be arrayed in fine linen, clean and bright, for the fine linen is the righteous acts of the saints. (Revelation 19:7–8 NKJV)

When God found us, we were orphans enslaved to sin and fear. Rather than punishing us for our sin and depravity, he poured his wrath out on Christ on the cross. In doing so, he purchased us out of slavery and began the process of transforming us into the beautiful, glorious bride-to-be presented before Christ at the marriage supper of the Lamb. What an amazing place we have been given in God's household! We are both children of the Sovereign Lord of the Universe and cherished bride of his firstborn Son. We occupy a high and honored position.

How should our lives reflect these truths? Kenosis, justification, and glorification must become more to us than just big theological words on paper. Does your life reflect an understanding of these doctrines? Have you forgiven the one who has hurt you, or do you demand that he or she pay in full for the offense? Are you still working to earn your own position before God? Or do you grasp daily all that Christ's death on the cross has purchased for you? Do you recognize the good work God is doing to transform you into his beautiful bride? Or do you resist and resent his work to change you?

We started with kenosis—Christ's emptying himself of his divine rights, letting go of his reputation, and humbling himself to the point of being crucified on the cross, the type of punishment administered to the worst criminals of that day. Compared to Christ, how do you view your rights and your reputation? Are you controlled by what others think about you? Have you mastered the art of subtle manipulation to manage how others view you? Many Christian women weigh their words, obsess over their clothes, and attempt to control big and small circumstances around them in an effort to build their reputation. They are constantly on guard for new strategies to make others think better of them. In contrast, we are called to humble ourselves—to forget ourselves, let go of our reputation and rights, and pour ourselves out in service to

Christ and others. Then we let Christ, rather than ourselves, take charge of our reputation and glorification. As we empty ourselves in humility, God transforms us, rooting out our sin and depravity and replacing it with character that reflects his own. We are commanded to allow the mind of Christ to rule over us in these matters, and his mind dictates that we give up our rights and think nothing of ourselves in our ministry to others.

10

We Are Connected to Jesus and Find Our Identity in Him

"I am the vine; you are the branches.
Whoever abides in me and I in him,
he it is that bears much fruit,
for apart from me you can do nothing."

—John 15:5

Where do you find your identity? If you have a blog or a MySpace page, what does it reveal about how you define yourself? How do you introduce yourself when someone asks, "What do you do?" I have been both a high-school and community-college math teacher, jobs in which I found a great deal of personal fulfillment. Now, I am the mother of two small boys, by far the most important and difficult job I have ever had. Often, I have looked to each role to feel good about myself, which leads to emotional devastation when I fail. God has used the role of wife and mom to finally get my attention on the issue of identity. My husband and boys can't be my idols. I can't pin all of my hopes for the future on their personal successes. It's not fair to them, and it keeps me from placing my hope for the future in God's hands. I must be a steward of my roles of wife and mom, not an idolater who looks to her husband and children for her sense of personal achievement. The same is true for you in whatever calling God has given you. Jesus must be our source of identity. But what exactly does it mean to find our identity in Christ?

The Bible uses many word pictures to communicate the details of our relationship with Christ. In the last chapter, we briefly explored our position as God's cherished bride, a word picture used to reflect our glorification. Unlike our male counterparts, most women begin valuing marriage at an early age and therefore appreciate the implications of picturing themselves as the bride of Christ. There are two more word pictures used in Scripture that teach us important truths about our identity in Christ: (1) Christ is the vine, and believers are the branches; (2) Christ is the head, and believers are his body.

Both of these analogies point to a very intimate union between Christ and his church. The Bible often talks about believers being *in Christ*, a phrase used about ninety times in the New Testament. Colossians 1:17 says that Christ is "before all things, and in him all things hold together." In other words, we can't get away from him. If you belong to God, then you and Christ are supernaturally connected. However, instead of seeing ourselves as connected to Christ at all times, we tend to view our relationship with God in terms of intersecting moments during the day. We think that the more times our lives intersect with God, the more "spiritual" we are. In this paradigm, God goes on his way and I go on my way until we intersect at another corner later that day, week, month, or year.

Instead, we need to think of ourselves walking with Jesus continually, twenty-four hours a day, seven days a week. If you are a believer, Christ is with you, in you, holding you together at all times. The goal is for us to be aware of that reality and live in light of it, for Christ warns us that apart from him we can do *nothing* (see John 15).

Vine and Branches

"I am the true vine, and My Father is the vinedresser. Every branch in Me that does not bear fruit He takes away; and every branch that bears fruit He prunes, that it may bear more fruit. . . . Abide in Me, and I in you. As the branch cannot bear fruit of itself, unless it abides in the vine, neither can you, unless you abide in Me. I am the vine, you are the branches. He who abides in Me, and I in him, bears much fruit; for without Me you can do nothing." (John 15:1–2, 4–5 NKJV)

Christ is the vine and we are the branches. We are supernaturally connected to Christ, and all of our strength and grace for overcoming with joy in this life flow from him. He is the root from which we get all of our sustenance for life. However, John 15 and other passages speak not only of the reality of our union with Christ, but also of *our need to meditate on and avail ourselves of the resources made available through this supernatural connection* (see Colossians 2). In other words, even though the Bible teaches that we are supernaturally connected to Christ, many believers continue to walk around oblivious to the power of this truth. Instead, we live as though we're orphans, completely dependent on ourselves.

Christ says, "Abide in me." The Greek word for *abide* is *menō*, meaning "to remain, tarry, be held, or kept continually."[1] All of us who know Christ as our Savior have the *opportunity* to dwell in his presence. His death on the cross purchased our freedom to boldly enter God's presence. But that doesn't mean that we do. We have access to God, but we just don't use it. Christ instructs us in John 15 to avail ourselves of the precious privilege his death on the cross purchased for us—the freedom to enter the presence of God. Abide in his presence. Remain in his presence. Meditate on your connection to him. The first temptation faced by all believers is the temptation to go to something or someone other than Christ for sustenance and encouragement. We go to sin, we go to people, or we go to experiences. Abiding in Christ and meditating on our connection with him becomes the last option to deal with our issues rather than the first. In reality, it is the only choice with any hope of real help.

John 15 uses the picture of a vine nourishing its attached branches. In Colossians 2, Paul continues the plant illustration, using the word "rooted" when discussing the benefits of our supernatural connection to Christ. Consider the benefits of living *in* Christ and being rooted *in* him as explained by the apostle Paul:

> Therefore, as you received Christ Jesus the Lord, so walk in him, rooted and built up in him and established in the faith, just as you were taught, abounding in thanksgiving. See to it that no one takes you captive by philosophy and empty deceit, according to human tradition, according to the elemental spirits of the world, and not according to Christ. For in him the whole fullness of deity dwells bodily, and you have been filled in him, who is the head of all rule and authority. (Colossians 2:6–10)

Dwelling in Christ

Paul emphasizes that not only are we rooted in Christ, but we must mentally take into account this truth and guard ourselves against deceptive thought patterns that take us captive and enslave us. We cannot overemphasize our need to *meditate* on these truths. We are going to be tempted to give in to thought patterns that reflect "human tradition" and "the elemental spirits of the world." We have to prayerfully focus on training our minds to dwell on Christ, in Christ, and with Christ. Christ is God. He is the head over every power and authority—and that's the power at our fingertips if we avail ourselves of his presence, set our minds on him, and live in light of our unity with him.

Paul discusses this in Ephesians 3, as well. Listen to his prayer as he encourages the Ephesians to *grasp*—comprehend and take hold of mentally—the truth of what they have in Christ:

> I pray that you, being rooted and established in love, may have power, together with all the saints, to grasp how wide and long and high and deep is the love of Christ, and to know this love that surpasses knowledge—that you may be filled to the measure of all the fullness of God. (Ephesians 3:17–19 NIV)

Paul often tells believers to take into account what they know to be true, to take their thoughts captive, and to set their minds on Christ and heavenly things. This is absolutely crucial to overcoming with joy despite our circumstances in life.

Some of us don't know the truth of the character of our God. But many more of us *do* know the truth but don't count on it, don't set our minds on it, don't take our thoughts captive and make them submit to it when we get to the practical issues of life. How often are we devastated, disappointed, or frustrated by problems that cloud our day and hang over our head? It may be as simple as getting a flat tire, more serious like losing a job, or the most serious issue of losing a loved one in death. What issue has put you in a bad mood? What situation is hanging over your head right now like a thunderous rain cloud? What thought patterns are governing your attitude? And are you going to allow those thought patterns to be your master, or are you going to take those thoughts captive and make them submit to what you know to be true about your God?

We are called to think this way: God is my sovereign, wise, and compassionate Father. He is intimately aware of the details of my life, and I can trust him with my circumstances. Christ took my sins on his shoulders to pave the way for me to enter God's presence. God is transforming me into Christ's image, and his discipline, his training in righteousness, is a blessing because it roots out sin and wrong thinking in my life. It is a very good thing that God doesn't leave me in the state he found me but transforms me, even when it involves hard circumstances. Christ is my perfect Bridegroom. The core longings of my heart for relationship are perfectly fulfilled in him. He loves me, he died for me, and he sits at the right hand of the Father eternally making intercession for me. These are the truths we are to count on throughout our day. For apart from abiding in Christ and meditating on the benefits of our relationship in him, we will be hamstrung in every attempt to handle life on our own. Apart from him, we can do nothing.

Head and Body

The other word picture of our unity with Christ is that he is the head and we are his body:

> He is the head of the body, the church. He is the beginning, the firstborn from the dead, that in everything he might be preeminent. (Colossians 1:18)

> And he put all things under his feet and gave him as head over all things to the church, which is his body, the fullness of him who fills all in all. (Ephesians 1:22–23)

Like the picture of a vine and branches, this analogy points to our supernatural connection to Jesus and our utter dependence upon him. A body has no power apart from its head. Most of us have witnessed someone struggle with quadriplegia, paralysis of the body from the neck down. When our body loses connection to our head, we can't feed ourselves, clothe ourselves, or control our movements. This is a perfect illustration of what happens spiritually when we are "not holding fast to the Head" (Colossians 2:19). We must hold fast to Jesus, abide in him, and take full advantage of the power available to us through our identity in him.

The Lord's Supper is designed to reflect this truth and cause us to meditate regularly on the connection we have to Jesus Christ. The bread is not for unbelievers. Only true believers are to eat the bread, reflecting on the fact that we, as members of the church, are participants in Christ's body.

> He took bread, and when he had given thanks, he broke it and gave it to them, saying, "This is my body, which is given for you. Do this in remembrance of me." (Luke 22:19)

> The cup of blessing that we bless, is it not a participation in the blood of Christ? The bread that we break, is it not a participation in the body of Christ? Because there is one bread, we who are many are one body, for we all partake of the one bread. (1 Corinthians 10:16–17)

Next time you receive the Lord's Supper, take time to meditate on the supernatural union we have with Christ himself. We are *in* him and he dwells *in* us. This union with Christ and our identity as his bride and body should define our responses to temptations and trials.

This picture of Christ as the head and believers as his body has implications for our relationship to the church as a whole as well.

Paul discusses this in Romans 12 and Ephesians 4, but we'll focus on his words to believers in Corinth in 1 Corinthians 12:

> For just as the body is one and has many members, and all the members of the body, though many, are one body, so it is with Christ. For in one Spirit we were all baptized into one body—Jews or Greeks, slaves or free—and all were made to drink of one Spirit.
>
> For the body does not consist of one member but of many. If the foot should say, "Because I am not a hand, I do not belong to the body," that would not make it any less a part of the body. And if the ear should say, "Because I am not an eye, I do not belong to the body," that would not make it any less a part of the body. If the whole body were an eye, where would be the sense of hearing? If the whole body were an ear, where would be the sense of smell? But as it is, God arranged the members in the body, each one of them, as he chose. If all were a single member, where would the body be? As it is, there are many parts, yet one body.
>
> The eye cannot say to the hand, "I have no need of you," nor again the head to the feet, "I have no need of you." On the contrary, the parts of the body that seem to be weaker are indispensable, and on those parts of the body that we think less honorable we bestow the greater honor, and our unpresentable parts are treated with greater modesty, which our more presentable parts do not require. But God has so composed the body, giving greater honor to the part that lacked it, that there may be no division in the body, but that the members may have the same care for one another. If one member suffers, all suffer together; if one member is honored, all rejoice together. Now you are the body of Christ and individually members of it. (1 Corinthians 12:12–27)

Christ and His Church

You and I are not only connected with the head, which is Christ, we are also connected to other members of Christ's body, which is the church. I love the closing line of Derek Webb's song "The

Church." Speaking as Christ, Webb sings, "You cannot live for Me with no regard for her. If you love Me, you will love the church." Webb makes an excellent point! Many believers claim to love Christ and abide in him, yet they attempt to separate their relationship with him from their relationship with his body, the church. "I love Christ, but the church gets on my nerves" isn't a reasonable excuse. We are members of Christ's body with mutual accountability and responsibility toward that body. We cannot serve the head and ignore the rest of his body. We need Christ's body as much as we need his head.

Does your life reflect this teaching of Scripture? Do you identify Christ as the head of your body and live like he is the brains of your operation? Does your life reflect the supernatural connection you have to the rest of his body? Are you living in community with your brothers and sisters in his body or in isolation from other believers? Does your relationship with the church show that you believe that you are members of one another, or do you disobey Paul's instructions by living as if you don't need the other members? It is not enough to have a head knowledge of these doctrines. We must examine ourselves daily to see if we live out these teachings. If not, we must take our thoughts captive and make them submit to the truth of God's Word.

For Further Study
Driscoll, Mark. *Vintage Jesus*. Wheaton, IL: Crossway Books, 2008.

11

God Is Our Help

Behold, God is my helper;
the LORD is the upholder of my life.

—Psalm 54:4

e've studied the character and attributes of God the Father. We've explored the word pictures painted in Scripture that describe our relationship with God the Son. However, in all of my study of theology, the Scripture we will soon read on God the Spirit has had the most profound impact on my interpersonal relationships, particularly in my marriage. I have come to have a deep appreciation for the person and work of the Spirit and hope you will also be changed by your study of him.

Who is the Holy Spirit? The Holy Spirit is God. He is equal with God the Father and God the Son, sharing the attributes of

God with both the Father and the Son. The Spirit has a specific role in the Trinity that includes submission to the Father and Son. It is important to note that the Spirit's willing submission in the Trinity does not imply that he is inferior to the Father or the Son. The Spirit plays a vital role in every believer's daily walk. God didn't save us and then leave us on our own to figure out the rest of the Christian life! God the Spirit now indwells us and leads us in repentance and in conformity to the example of God the Son, Jesus Christ.[1]

Rather than giving details on *who* the Spirit *is*, the Scripture speaks more of *what* the Spirit *does*. The Bible enlightens us to the character and work of the Holy Spirit mainly through the names that are given to him and the descriptions of his role by Jesus and the apostle Paul. Consider the following Scripture passages that give specific names for the Spirit.

Deposit, Guarantee, and Seal

Now it is God who makes both us and you stand firm in Christ. He anointed us, set his seal of ownership on us, and put his Spirit in our hearts as a deposit, guaranteeing what is to come. (2 Corinthians 1:21–22 NIV)

In Him you also trusted, after you heard the word of truth, the gospel of your salvation; in whom also, having believed, you were sealed with the Holy Spirit of promise, who is the guarantee of our inheritance until the redemption of the purchased possession, to the praise of His glory. (Ephesians 1:13–14 NKJV)

God the Spirit is described as the deposit, guarantee, and seal of our salvation. Consider the meaning of these descriptions of the Holy Spirit:

- Deposit: "A payment given as a guarantee that an obligation will be met."
- Guarantee: "Something that assures a particular outcome or condition; a pledge that something will be performed in a specified manner."
- Seal: "Anything that serves as assurance, confirmation, or bond."[2]

If you are a believer, the Holy Spirit lives in you as a guarantee of your salvation. Paul teaches that "anyone who does not have the Spirit of Christ does not belong to him" (Romans 8:9). All believers have the Spirit as a seal upon their hearts. Between the time we accept Christ as our Savior and see the fulfillment of our salvation in heaven, the Spirit remains in us as God's deposit, assuring us that God will not default on his promises. This is a precious gift from God. He hasn't left us as orphans. Instead, he lives within us so that we may be confident that our relationship with him is permanent and effective.

Comforter, Counselor, Helper

The Holy Spirit is also called the Comforter (KJV), Counselor (NIV), or Helper (ESV). These are the English translations of the Greek word *paraklētos*, which means "to call to one's aid, to counsel, to plead another's case before a judge, to intercede on another's behalf, to help, assist, or nourish." Christ teaches us a lot about the Holy Spirit's role as the *paraclete* in John 14, 15, and 16:

> "If you love me, you will keep my commandments. And I will ask the Father, and he will give you another Helper, to be with you forever, even the Spirit of truth, whom the world cannot receive, because it neither sees him nor knows him. You know him, for he dwells with you and will be in you. I will not leave you as orphans;

I will come to you. . . . But the Helper, the Holy Spirit, whom the Father will send in my name, he will teach you all things and bring to your remembrance all that I have said to you." (John 14:15–18, 26)

"But when the Helper comes, whom I will send to you from the Father, the Spirit of truth, who proceeds from the Father, he will bear witness about me." (John 15:26)

"Nevertheless, I tell you the truth: it is to your advantage that I go away, for if I do not go away, the Helper will not come to you. But if I go, I will send him to you. And when he comes, he will convict the world concerning sin and righteousness and judgment: concerning sin, because they do not believe in me; concerning righteousness, because I go to the Father, and you will see me no longer; concerning judgment, because the ruler of this world is judged. I still have many things to say to you, but you cannot bear them now. When the Spirit of truth comes, he will guide you into all the truth, for he will not speak on his own authority, but whatever he hears he will speak, and he will declare to you the things that are to come. He will glorify me, for he will take what is mine and declare it to you." (John 16:7–14)

Notice what Christ says in John 16:7: "It is to your advantage that I go away." At times I have longed to physically sit at Jesus' feet as his disciples did. However, Christ indicates that we have a privilege that exceeds that of the disciples. The Holy Spirit, God himself, lives inside of us at all times in all locations as our comforter, counselor, and helper. As wonderful as it would have been to walk and talk with Jesus during his earthly ministry, we have even greater access to God today through the Holy Spirit's constant presence and counsel in our lives. What a wonderful privilege this is!

Note also that the Spirit's job is to "convict the world concerning sin" (John 16:8). In particular, the Spirit guides us "into all the truth" (v. 13). He convicts us of our need for salvation, reminds us of the teachings of Christ, and guides us into all truth until we see God face-to-face in eternity. He is our consistent, permanent counselor. About what does the Spirit counsel us? Christ teaches that the Spirit does not elevate himself. Christ says the Spirit "will not speak on his own authority" and "he will glorify me" (vv. 13–14). What does this mean for us today? This teaches us the key to recognizing a ministry that is controlled by the Holy Spirit. Such ministries center themselves on the name of Christ and obedience to his teachings. If a ministry talks more about the Holy Spirit than it does about Christ, it is probably not controlled by the Spirit of God. The Spirit is all about Christ rather than himself. The best way to figure out if a ministry is controlled by the Holy Spirit is to evaluate the clarity of its teaching and worship of Christ.

In the book of Romans, the apostle Paul gives us more insight into the comforting, helping role of the Spirit: "Likewise the Spirit helps us in our weakness. For we do not know what to pray for as we ought, but the Spirit himself intercedes for us with groanings too deep for words" (Romans 8:26). Not only does the Holy Spirit counsel us with the teachings of Christ, but he also pleads our case in heaven, groaning our plight before God even when our situation is too painful for words. Have you been in a situation where you could not even begin to articulate your prayers? There have been times in my life when I was so overwhelmed by circumstances that I could not have formulated a prayer if my life depended on it. How encouraging it is to know that the Holy Spirit faithfully helps us in our times of weakness, coming before God on our behalf to groan our plight.

Let's summarize the main ideas we have gleaned from the names the Scripture uses for the Holy Spirit. First, we saw that the Holy Spirit is God's seal upon us, guaranteeing that "he who began a good work in you will bring it to completion at the day of Jesus Christ" (Philippians 1:6). In other words, we can have confidence that the God who saved us from our sinful condition will continue to transform us into the image of Christ until he presents us in our completely transformed state in heaven. Second, the Spirit is our Counselor, our Comforter, and our Helper, given by God to convict us of sin and remind us twenty-four hours a day, seven days a week of the teachings of Jesus Christ in this process of transformation. The Spirit not only counsels us in the teachings of Christ, he also intercedes for us before God in heaven as our advocate.

Filled with the Spirit

> Do not get drunk with wine, for that is debauchery, but be filled with the Spirit. (Ephesians 5:18)

While all believers are indwelt by the Holy Spirit and sealed by him, not all believers act consistently with his control. The Scripture exhorts believers, even though they are *sealed* with the Spirit, also to be *filled* with the Spirit. This means that we yield to him without grieving, quenching, or resisting.

Two other passages give us insight into the difference between being filled with the Spirit and being resistant to the Spirit. The Bible also warns us against quenching the Holy Spirit in 1 Thessalonians 5:19 and against grieving the Holy Spirit in Ephesians 4:30. Consider the context of Paul's words in Ephesians 4:

> Let no corrupting talk come out of your mouths, but only such as is good for building up, as fits the occasion, that it may give grace to those who hear. And do not grieve the Holy Spirit of God, by whom you were sealed for the day of redemption. Let all bitterness

and wrath and anger and clamor and slander be put away from you, along with all malice. Be kind to one another, tenderhearted, forgiving one another, as God in Christ forgave you. (Ephesians 4:29–32)

Notice that the warning in Ephesians 4 against grieving the Spirit is given in the context of the use of angry, bitter language. We are called to put away slander (the abusive attack on a person's character or good name) and bitterness (conversation marked by resentment, cynicism, anger, or ill will). In place of it, we are commanded to be kind, compassionate, and forgiving *just as Christ forgave us* (see also Colossians 3:12–13). Is it any wonder that angry and bitter communication grieves, causes sorrow, and offends the Holy Spirit? When we repeat evil reports against one another or participate in bitter speech, we spit upon God's grace poured out on us. The way we use our tongues reflects Christ's teaching that "out of the abundance of the heart the mouth speaks" (Matthew 12:34). Though there are many indicators of a heart that resists the Spirit, the use of destructive speech in our homes, churches, marriages, and friendships is a definite red flag.

In this chapter, we have focused on the implications of the descriptions and names Scripture uses for the Holy Spirit—deposit, seal, guarantee, Comforter, Counselor, and Helper. The Holy Spirit is God's deposit in us that assures us he will not default on his promises to us. The Spirit is our comforter and counselor as we are conformed to the image of Christ through the rest of our earthly lives. As you meditate on the role of the Holy Spirit, consider how understanding him should impact your daily life. I have been greatly impacted by learning about the Spirit's role of counselor. His job is to convict the world of sin and remind us of Christ's teachings, and he is very good at his job. We can trust God the Spirit to convict men of sin. This has been a powerful doctrine to remember in conflicts, especially within marriage. Many times I

v. nag

To constantly scold, criticize, or complain in an effort to change behavior.

v. manipulate

To control through covert or devious methods.

have been tempted to nag and manipulate my husband to come around to my way of thinking on a particular issue. However, I must guard my tongue and let no unwholesome conversation come out of my mouth. In the midst of conflict, I can pray to God and trust his ability to convict my husband of sin. The Spirit has consistently shown himself quite capable of this. Sometimes he convicts my husband. Many times he convicts me of my own wrong thinking. But opening my mouth and letting out angry speech has never once contributed to reconciliation. Instead, it has grieved and quenched the Spirit. The right response is to shut my mouth, pray for transformation, and rest in what I know to be true of the Holy Spirit. Faith in God's character and trust in the Spirit's ability to convict men of sin is a powerful force for reconciliation in our relationships.

The Spirit Sanctifies Us

We all, with unveiled face,
beholding the glory of the Lord,
are being transformed into the same image
from one degree of glory to another.
For this comes from the Lord who is the Spirit.

—2 Corinthians 3:18

Earlier, we discussed Christ's role in our justification. Justification is the act in which God declares us righteous in heaven by switching our sins to Christ's shoulders and Christ's righteousness to ours. Sanctification, which follows justification, is the day-to-day process whereby we slowly become in reality what God has already declared us to be in heaven (i.e., completely righteous).

Regeneration is our birth in Christ. Sanctification is our growth in Christ. At birth, we are forgiven for our sins, released from guilt for our depraved acts, and freed from our slavery to sin. And yet, even after our new birth, we are still sinners. Now that we are released from slavery to sin through our salvation (see Romans 6:6–7), we learn to "put to death" (Colossians 3:5) the members of our body that continue to sin as we grow in Christ.

The Holy Spirit is the primary influence in our sanctification. In fact, one of the Holy Spirit's major functions as part of the Trinity is facilitating the process of sanctification in believers' lives. The Bible refers to this in 2 Thessalonians 2:13 and 1 Peter 1:2 as the "sanctifying work of the Spirit" (NIV).

> **n. sanctification**
>
> Becoming in reality what you are already declared to be by God in Christ.

In the last chapter we looked at descriptions of the Spirit's work and biblical names for the Spirit. Consider how those descriptions—deposit, seal, and guarantee—and names—Counselor, Comforter, and Helper—apply to the process of sanctification. Christ broke the bonds that enslaved us to sin. Now, the Holy Spirit lives in us, counseling us in the teachings of Christ, convicting us of sin in our lives, and transforming us slowly and steadily into the image of Christ. As our deposit, seal, and guarantee, the Holy Spirit assures us of God's promises, sin's enslaving power over us is officially broken, and our position in Christ is secure.

Multiple Realities

In 2 Corinthians 4, the apostle Paul gives insight into the opposing forces at work in a believer's life:

> For what we proclaim is not ourselves, but Jesus Christ as Lord, with ourselves as your servants for Jesus' sake. For God, who said, "Let light shine out of darkness," has shone in our hearts to give the light of the knowledge of the glory of God in the face of Jesus Christ But we have this treasure in jars of clay, to show that the surpassing power belongs to God and not to us. We are afflicted in every way,

but not crushed; perplexed, but not driven to despair; persecuted, but not forsaken; struck down, but not destroyed; always carrying in the body the death of Jesus, so that the life of Jesus may also be manifested in our bodies. . . . So we do not lose heart. Though our outer self is wasting away, our inner self is being renewed day by day. For this light momentary affliction is preparing for us an eternal weight of glory beyond all comparison, as we look not to the things that are seen but to the things that are unseen. For the things that are seen are transient, but the things that are unseen are eternal. (2 Corinthians 4:5–10, 16–18)

We have an outward, earthly reality in which we're perplexed, persecuted, and wasting away. I doubt I have to convince many of you of the truth of that statement. In contrast, we also have an inward, eternal reality that reflects our sanctification, God's renewal and transformation of our depraved souls into children who mirror God's glory. It is not natural for us to focus on what God is doing on the inside, but if we are to have any hope of enduring our earthly reality, then we need to "fix our eyes" on this internal reality.

Finally, we have a heavenly reality where our standing before God is eternally secured by Christ's death on the cross. The goal is to mesh these into one consistent perspective through which we view all the issues of life. On earth, I'm bruised and beaten by external forces. In heaven, Christ has secured a place for me in God's presence for eternity. Sanctification is the transformation between the two. The outward man is dying while the inner man is being renewed in light of the eternal position secured for me in heaven.

The Bible has interesting ways of revealing the workings of the Spirit in this inner transformation. How does sanctification happen? We are also tempted to ask, "Who does the work: the Holy Spirit or me?" But that's the wrong question. It's not an either/or proposition in which either the Spirit transforms me and I lay back passively, or I do all the work by regulating and transforming myself. Consider how Scripture speaks of this concept:

> "Consecrate yourselves and be holy, because I am the LORD your God. Keep my decrees and follow them. I am the LORD, who makes you holy." (Leviticus 20:7–8 NIV)

> Therefore, my beloved, as you have always obeyed, so now, not only as in my presence but much more in my absence, work out your own salvation with fear and trembling, for it is God who works in you, both to will and to work for his good pleasure. (Philippians 2:12–13)

In Leviticus 20 we're commanded to be holy (sanctified or set apart for God's purposes) because God is making us holy. In Philippians 2 we're told to work out what God is working in. Our growth in righteousness is accomplished by a relationship with God that results in an outward transformation that reflects the Spirit's inner working in our hearts. The Holy Spirit is working in and with me, so that I show outwardly what he is changing in me. Any righteousness we exhibit outwardly is a result of our inner relationship with the Spirit. You can't separate the two.

Transformed by the Spirit

How does the Spirit transform us? The Spirit's primary instrument of sanctification is the Word of God. As he is praying to God the Father, Christ says, "Sanctify them in the truth; your word is truth" (John 17:17). Even our study of the Word is a joint venture with the Holy Spirit. The longest chapter in the Bible, Psalm 119, is dedicated to the power and beauty of the Word. Note the psalmist's prayer in verse 18:

> Open my eyes, that I may behold
> wondrous things out of your law.

The psalmist knew that after a lifetime of being blinded by sin, he was dependent on God to open his eyes to see the truth. As we read the Word of God, we too must pray that the Spirit would enable us to see the truth of Scripture. Once our eyes are open to the truth, the Spirit then begins the process of transforming our thinking and actions to reflect the truth found in the Word.

Finally, there are forces working against us in our sanctification, our growth in righteousness, and conformity to the image of Christ. The Scriptures warn us of two external enemies in particular: Satan and the cares of this world:

> Be sober-minded; be watchful. Your adversary the devil prowls around like a roaring lion, seeking someone to devour. (1 Peter 5:8)

> "The one who received the seed that fell among the thorns is the man who hears the word, but the worries of this life and the deceitfulness of wealth choke it, making it unfruitful. But the one who received the seed that fell on good soil is the man who hears the word and understands it. He produces a crop, yielding a hundred, sixty or thirty times what was sown." (Matthew 13:22–23 NIV)

Enemies to Growth

Satan is our enemy in our growth in Christ. Though Christ has defeated him on the cross, Satan still seeks to destroy anyone he finds vulnerable. Peter warns us to be "sober-minded" and "watchful." In other words, we need to be aware of Satan's desire to destroy us and then discipline ourselves in preparation for his attacks.

Our other external enemy is twofold: the worries of this life and the deceitfulness of wealth. I would sum up this enemy with the phrase "surface-level distractions." These are the things in our lives we can see that distract us from the greater, deeper things God is working for us in places we cannot see. We have heard the

Word, we have seen from Scripture the character of God and his plan for our righteousness and his glory, but we are distracted away from him by some situation in our lives. Instead of the circumstance causing us to cling deeply to him and to meditate on our relationship with him, we allow it to divert our focus away from him. Your car needs unexpected repairs, an inconvenience that disrupts and complicates your well-planned day. On top of that, you have to spend money you had set aside for other real needs. But your God is sovereign, compassionate, and wise. He loves you and has plans for you set in motion from before time began. Do you allow these truths to interpret your circumstances, or do you allow your circumstances to distract you from these truths? The first option leads to fruit. The second choice strangles us.

We are called to set our minds on heavenly things, to take our thoughts captive and submit to the truth of the Word, and to keep our minds set steadfastly on God (see Colossians 3:1; 2 Corinthians 10:5; and Isaiah 26:3). In other words, our focus is to be on the eternal—heaven, Christ, and the kingdom of God. We are choked from fruitfulness when we become consumed with the cares of this temporary world and, in particular, the deceitfulness of riches. We talked in an earlier chapter about the problem of being more convinced of the reality of our daily problems than the reality of our God. We will never be fruitful for the Savior if we fail to look past our surface-level, earthly cares to see the heavenly reality beneath.

Along with the external enemies of our growth in Christ, we also have the internal enemy of the flesh, or "old man."

The desires of the flesh are against the Spirit, and the desires of the Spirit are against the flesh, for these are opposed to each other, to keep you from doing the things you want to do. (Galatians 5:17)

What shall we say then? Are we to continue in sin that grace may abound? By no means! How can we who died to sin still live in it?

. . . We know that our old self was crucified with him in order that the body of sin might be brought to nothing, so that we would no longer be enslaved to sin. For one who has died has been set free from sin. Now if we have died with Christ, we believe that we will also live with him. We know that Christ, being raised from the dead, will never die again; death no longer has dominion over him. For the death he died he died to sin, once for all, but the life he lives he lives to God. So you also must consider yourselves dead to sin and alive to God in Christ Jesus. Let not sin therefore reign in your mortal body, to make you obey its passions. (Romans 6:1–2, 6–12)

Fighting the Battle
How do we fight the external enemies of Satan and the world and the internal enemy of the old man? We need to know who we are in Christ, believe what we know to be true, and obey. We just read in Romans 6:11 Paul's exhortation to "consider yourselves dead to sin and alive to God in Christ Jesus." We have to mentally review our doctrine and live obediently in light of it. We do not do our part alone—the Spirit enables us.

I pray that out of his glorious riches he may strengthen you with power through his Spirit in your inner being. (Ephesians 3:16 NIV)

I have been crucified with Christ. It is no longer I who live, but Christ who lives in me. And the life I now live in the flesh I live by faith in the Son of God, who loved me and gave himself for me. I do not nullify the grace of God, for if righteousness were through the law, then Christ died for no purpose. O foolish Galatians! Who has bewitched you? It was before your eyes that Jesus Christ was publicly portrayed as crucified. Let me ask you only this: Did you receive the Spirit by works of the law or by hearing with faith? Are you so foolish? Having begun by the Spirit, are you now being perfected by the flesh? (Galatians 2:20–3:3)

Paul gives a good summary of this entire concept in his letter to the church at Philippi:

> Not that I have already obtained this or am already perfect, but I press on to make it my own, because Christ Jesus has made me his own. Brothers, I do not consider that I have made it my own. But one thing I do: forgetting what lies behind and straining forward to what lies ahead, I press on toward the goal for the prize of the upward call of God in Christ Jesus. Let those of us who are mature think this way, and if in anything you think otherwise, God will reveal that also to you.... Brothers, join in imitating me, and keep your eyes on those who walk according to the example you have in us. For many, of whom I have often told you and now tell you even with tears, walk as enemies of the cross of Christ. Their end is destruction, their god is their belly, and they glory in their shame, with minds set on earthly things. But our citizenship is in heaven, and from it we await a Savior, the Lord Jesus Christ, who will transform our lowly body to be like his glorious body, by the power that enables him even to subject all things to himself. (Philippians 3:12–15, 17–21)

This is sanctification, our transformation into Christ's image. We press on to take hold of the things that Christ's death on the cross has purchased for us. We keep our eyes on the goal to which God has called us. And while those around us may be consumed with earthly cares, we meditate on our citizenship in heaven and eagerly await our face-to-face meeting with our Savior, Jesus Christ. We set our mind on him, abide in him, and then reflect on the outside what he is working on the inside.

For Further Study

Stott, John R. W. *Baptism and Fullness: The Work of the Holy Spirit Today* (Downers Grove, IL: InterVarsity, 1976).

Part *three*

Communicating with Our God

We have studied the character and attributes of God the Father, Son, and Spirit. However, there is a difference between knowing *about* God and knowing him personally. Head knowledge of God is of no value if it is not connected to a personal relationship with him, and relationship with God demands communication with him.

God has not left us to figure him out all by ourselves. He invites us to dialogue with him about his character and purposes. He stands ready to reveal himself to us. He is also equipped to reveal our own heart back to us. Therefore, we must answer the question, "How do we communicate with God?"

Prayer Is Our Means
of Conversing with God

Rejoice always, pray without ceasing,
give thanks in all circumstances;
for this is the will of God in Christ Jesus for you.

—1 Thessalonians 5:16–18

We'll start with prayer, which is our means of conversation with God. As we just read, for those of us *in* Christ, it is God's will that we pray without ceasing. Does that sound like a heavy burden? Does God really expect me to talk with him all day? I've got groceries to buy, kids to feed, tests to study for, and bosses to please. I don't have time to pray all day long. If you think that way, remember what we learned about our connection with Jesus in earlier chapters. You and I are *in* Christ and commanded to *abide* with Christ. Christ is the head and we are his body. When we are at the grocery store, school, home, or work, we are supernaturally connected with Christ all day, every day. We have God Almighty living in us as the Spirit, and we are called to reflect this reality and take advantage of it in the form of prayer. Sometimes it will be a gushing river of conversation with God, flowing through the forefront of our minds. Sometimes it will be a quiet stream of meditation and rest in the background of our minds. Regardless, we should always walk mindful of God's presence. We all know what it's like to have something on our mind all day. Well, God is to be on our mind continually. We are called to constantly acknowledge and take advantage of the supernatural union we have with God Almighty.

The Lord's Prayer

What should prayer consist of? Contrary to popular thought among some Christians, the prayer of Jabez in 1 Chronicles was not given to us as our model for prayer. Rather, Jesus gave us our model for prayer when he responded to his disciples' question about how to pray. The model he gave them, the Lord's Prayer, is recorded in both Luke 11 and Matthew 6. We'll examine the Matthew 6 passage here:

> "When you pray, do not heap up empty phrases as the Gentiles do, for they think that they will be heard for their many words. Do not be like them, for your Father knows what you need before you ask him. Pray then like this:
>
> > Our Father in heaven,
> > > hallowed be your name.
> > > Your kingdom come,
> > > your will be done,
> > > > on earth as it is in heaven.

Give us this day our daily bread,
and forgive us our debts,
    as we also have forgiven our debtors.
And lead us not into temptation,
    but deliver us from evil. (Matthew 6:7–13)

Hallowed

Christ begins with "hallowed be your name." The word *hallowed* is the Greek word *hagiazo*. It means to set apart as holy, to respect, honor, and greatly revere. The word *name* indicates everything that the name covers; every thought or feeling that is aroused in the mind by mentioning the name.

In his name the Gentiles will hope. (Matthew 12:21)

"Go therefore and make disciples of all nations, baptizing them in the name of the Father and of the Son and of the Holy Spirit." (Matthew 28:19)

For this reason also, God highly exalted Him, and bestowed on Him the name which is above every name, so that at the name of Jesus EVERY KNEE WILL BOW, of those who are in heaven and on earth and under the earth. (Philippians 2:9–10 NASB)

Christ teaches us to open our prayers to the Father with a cry for the holiness of God's name so that everything for which his name stands will be set apart and esteemed as special and worthy. "Father, I want to see your name lifted up, set apart, and held in the esteem that it deserves."

God's Kingdom

The next phrase Christ uses to teach the disciples how to pray is "Your kingdom come." What exactly is the kingdom of God? The

Roman Catholic Church teaches that the kingdom of God is fulfilled through the Catholic Church here on earth. In contrast, many evangelical Christians see the kingdom of God as something entirely in the future, marked by the return of Christ and his triumph at the battle of Armageddon. Both of these views tend to miss the parallel ways the Bible talks about God's kingdom. We know from Matthew 3:2 that Christ's incarnation marked the coming of the kingdom. Here John the Baptist announces that "the kingdom of God is at hand," linking the coming of God's kingdom with the earthly ministry of Christ. But did Christ's earthly ministry usher in all of the benefits of the kingdom? Is this as good as it gets? In Hebrews 2, the author uses Psalm 8 to explain that there are two parts to the fulfillment of the kingdom:

> "You made him for a little while lower than the angels;
>   you have crowned him with glory and honor,
>   putting everything in subjection under his feet."
>
> Now in putting everything in subjection to him, he left nothing outside his control. (Hebrews 2:7–8)

Christ is king, and all of creation is subject to him—the kingdom of God is truly at hand. And yet we have experienced only the first fruits of this kingdom; we haven't yet seen "everything in subjection under his feet." We have great expectations for the future as we anticipate the full benefits of being a child of the king. Wayne Grudem explains:

> There is a close connection between the kingdom of God and the church. As the church proclaims the good news of the kingdom, people will come into the church and begin to experience the blessings of God's rule in their lives. The kingdom manifests itself

through the church, and thereby the future reign of God breaks into the present.[1]

What does this phrase from the Lord's Prayer mean for us? This is not just a prayer for some far-off end-times event to occur. Rather, it's a prayer that God's kingdom will be evident in our lives and that his royal authority would permeate our world. Our prayer is that submission to his name would spread further and further and deeper and deeper into the nations and cultures of the world.

God's Will Be Done

So far we've been instructed to pray for God's name to be honored and his kingdom to grow. The next phrase is "your will be done on earth as it is in heaven." We now pray, "God, I want your will, purposes, and desires to be accomplished on earth as quickly and thoroughly as the angels accomplish them in heaven."

How exactly is God's will done in heaven? Christ says in Matthew 26:53 (NASB), "Do you think that I cannot appeal to My Father, and He will at once put at My disposal more than twelve legions of angels?" When God speaks his will in heaven, it is immediately obeyed. The angels stand ready to accomplish God's purposes. Our prayer should be that we on earth would respond as quickly and fully to God's desires as the angels do in heaven.

Daily Bread

Christ next instructs with the phrase, "Give us this day our daily bread." The three previous supplications in the Lord's Prayer centered on God's name, God's will, and God's glory. We often get this backward in our prayers. We often think of prayer as a wish list to dictate to our personal genie. But prayer is first and foremost praise and adoration to the One who has purchased our salvation for us. It's only after praising him and praying that his purposes be accomplished that God then invites us to bring our requests before him.

Matthew 6:8 says that "your Father knows what you need before you ask him." The issue is not that we must bring God our laundry list of needs lest he be unaware of them. No, God allows us to bring him our requests partly so that we will have peace of mind:

> Do not be anxious about anything, but in everything by prayer and supplication with thanksgiving let your requests be made known to God. And the peace of God, which surpasses all understanding, will guard your hearts and your minds in Christ Jesus. (Philippians 4:6–7)

God invites us to bring our requests to him because time spent in his presence in prayer is a means of experiencing his grace. God promises supernatural peace to stabilize our hearts and minds when we bring our needs to him. We don't bring our needs to him for his benefit but for ours. This truth was especially obvious to me when my husband and I were having problems getting pregnant again after miscarrying our first child. I remember well the despair that came with each negative pregnancy test. There was one time when, for weeks, I had talked myself into thinking I was pregnant. Was that a hint of nausea? My period was a half-day late after all. When I got back a negative result, I wanted to throw the stained stick against the bathroom wall. As I sat morosely in our home office, my husband tried to engage me on the subject. Honestly, he didn't struggle with the issue the way I did, but he knew that it deeply bothered me. Even so, he didn't know how to encourage me. Finally, after a few attempts, he asked me to consider what God had taught us about himself over the years. Then he simply prayed with me. His prayer wasn't long or complicated. But when I got up from that prayer, I felt a peace I had definitely not felt when I first bowed my head.

My peace wasn't centered on a conviction that God was going to make me pregnant soon. It was a simpler peace—God was good, and I could trust him. God ministered to me through that simple prayer.

Forgiven Debts

The next phrase Christ gives us in Matthew 6 is "forgive us our debts, as we also have forgiven our debtors." Forgiveness is a concept often discussed in Scripture.

> "Whenever you stand praying, forgive, if you have anything against anyone, so that your Father who is in heaven will also forgive you your transgressions." (Mark 11:25 NASB)

> Be kind to one another, tenderhearted, forgiving one another, as God in Christ forgave you. (Ephesians 4:32)

When we forgive others, it reflects what God has done for us on the cross. We're not talking about forgiving someone for some minor offense; we're talking about forgiveness that requires letting go of legitimate bitterness and anger. Someone really has done you wrong. That person has seriously hurt you. And based on what Christ has done for us on the cross, we have only *one* choice. We must respond to him or her as Christ has responded to us—returning kindness for evil, forgiving instead of harboring bitterness and anger.

This is an absolute requirement for prayer. Remember, the only reason we are allowed to enter God's presence with our requests is that Christ bore our sins on the cross, and God placed Christ's righteousness in our accounts, which is all of *grace*. How can we then enter God's presence based on this grace while being unwilling to extend it to the next guy? Such an attitude mocks what Christ has done for us on the cross.

Delivered from Evil

The final phrase in Christ's instructive prayer is "lead us not into temptation, but deliver us from evil." We often make the mistake of thinking that, while Christ was fully responsible for our rescue from sin at the time of our salvation, it is up to us to figure out how to battle temptation for the rest of our lives. In reality, we are utterly dependent on God in our battle to put to death our sinful desires and grow more and more like Christ. The apostle Paul encourages the Corinthians with this truth:

> No temptation has overtaken you but such as is common to man; and God is faithful, who will not allow you to be tempted beyond what you are able, but with the temptation will provide the way of escape also, so that you will be able to endure it. (1 Corinthians 10:13 NASB)

The implication here is that our battle with temptation is a joint venture with God. Peter teaches that "the Lord knows how to rescue the godly from temptation" (2 Peter 2:9 NASB). After we are saved, you and I are no longer slaves to sin. God promises that when we are presented with a temptation to sin, he will provide a way of escape so that we may bear it. He makes the way of escape, and we are obligated to walk closely with him so that we might both recognize and take advantage of the escape he provides for us. We are dependent upon God, in prayer, for this. In the Christian life we cannot overcome sin apart from continually seeking out God's presence in prayer.

In summary, Christ instructs us to pray to the Father, focusing on his name, his kingdom, and his purposes. He then instructs us to seek God's face concerning our daily needs and temptations, all within the framework of God's forgiveness of us, which leads to our forgiveness of others.

Persevering in Prayer

Later Christ gives a parable to teach his disciples to persevere in prayer:

> He told them a parable to the effect that they ought always to pray and not lose heart. He said, "In a certain city there was a judge who neither feared God nor respected man. And there was a widow in that city who kept coming to him and saying, 'Give me justice against my adversary.' For a while he refused, but afterward he said to himself, 'Though I neither fear God nor respect man, yet because this widow keeps bothering me, I will give her justice, so that she will not beat me down by her continual coming.'" And the Lord said, "Hear what the unrighteous judge says. And will not God give justice to his elect, who cry to him day and night? Will he delay long over them? I tell you, he will give justice to them speedily." (Luke 18:1–8)

I love this parable. God is inviting us to nag him in prayer! We know he is already aware of our needs and has a plan to meet them, yet we see again that he invites us to bring our concerns and worries to him. Why? Because God knows that praying to him keeps our hearts and minds at peace. As much as prayer is incense to God, it is also God's ministry to us. He knows that we are frail, and we become anxious with worry. He instructs us that praying to him, coming to him in faith, and leaving our requests at his feet is the antidote for worry.

When we are overcome with fear and worry, how often do we seek out friends, family, or church leaders to unburden ourselves? We feel this overwhelming need to pour out our hearts to someone, but we so often ignore the One to whom we should be pouring out our hearts. Pouring out our requests before God is the number one way to deal with vexing issues. It is the most effective way to mentally deal with our burdens. But few of us act as if we believe Scripture about this. Remember Paul's words in Philippians 4:6–7:

> Do not be anxious about anything, but in everything by prayer and supplication with thanksgiving let your requests be made known to God. And the peace of God, which surpasses all understanding, will guard your hearts and your minds in Christ Jesus.

This is not a trite, feel-good saying. It is the truth of God. We need to think through Paul's exhortation and evaluate our lives to see if we live as though we believe it is true.

In summary, we are called to "pray without ceasing" (1 Thessalonians 5:17). Christ has given us a model for prayer in Matthew 6 and Luke 11. This model begins with a focus on God's glory and God's will. Praise of him must precede our petitions for ourselves. But he does invite our requests! He wants us to lay our burdens at his feet and allow him to carry the heavy weight of our baggage, and he promises supernatural peace that passes our ability to understand when we present our requests to him with praise and thanksgiving.

14

What Is the Word?

So faith comes from hearing,
and hearing through the word of Christ.

—Romans 10:17

*W*e established in chapter 12 that the Word of God is the Spirit's primary instrument for our transformation into Christlikeness:

> The word of God is living and active, sharper than any two-edged sword, piercing to the division of soul and of spirit, of joints and of marrow, and discerning the thoughts and intentions of the heart. (Hebrews 4:12)

> "Is not my word like fire, declares the LORD, and like a hammer that breaks the rock in pieces?" (Jeremiah 23:29)

The Greek word for the Word of God is *logos*. From it, our modern culture has coined the term *logo*, a picture representing a company or product. Consider the implications of a company's logo on its letterhead. The logo implies that there is a much larger corporate structure backing up anything printed on the letterhead. Logos tend to be trademarked and protected because when the logo is used, it reflects the vision and philosophy of particular people—the company's executives, shareholders, and employees. In a much deeper way, God's Word, God's *logos*, represents him. It is the primary way throughout the ages that he has identified and expressed himself. In Hebrews 1, the author says that God has expressed himself "in these last days" through the person of Jesus Christ (v. 2). All of our knowledge of Christ, the *Logos*, is contained in the written Word of God, the Bible. So in our pursuit of God, it is crucial that we understand and avail ourselves of his expression of himself in his Word.

Living and Active

We read in Hebrews 4:12 that the Word of God is "living and active." It pierces our hearts and discerns our thoughts and intentions. *Nothing* will open our eyes to our needs and enable us to correct wrong thinking as will the Word of God itself. As Jeremiah says, God's Word is "like a hammer" that can break the hardest hearts. Any power in a sermon or good spiritual book stems from God working first and foremost through his Word.

"All Scripture is breathed out by God and profitable for teaching, for reproof, for correction, and for training in righteousness, that the man of God may be competent, equipped for every good work" (2 Timothy 3:16–17). All Scripture is inspired by God, not invented by human reasoning, and is useful for four key things: it teaches us what is right, rebukes us when we are wrong, corrects us when we are heading in the wrong direction, and, finally, trains us to stay on the righteous path. Paul ends this passage by saying that

Scripture is able to fully equip all believers for "every good work" to which God has called them. This is a phrase on which we need to meditate. Do I believe that the Word of God alone contains God's complete instructions to me and that it is sufficient to equip me fully for every action to which he has called me?

Personally, I have to fight the tendency to place the Word of God down in third place on my priority list, after wise counselors and good Christian books. I find it easier to seek wisdom from people or books rather than from God himself in his Word. However, this attitude works against me in the very areas I need help. No Christian book can claim to be the hammer that breaks the heart of stone. No wise counselor can claim the ability to judge the unspoken attitudes of our hearts. Only God's Word has this type of power, and we must avail ourselves of his revelation to us through his written Word.

The Word Reveals Christ

What does the Word of God reveal about God himself? In John 5:39, Christ rebukes the Jews, saying that they have studied the Old Testament diligently in an attempt to gain eternal life but have missed that the Scriptures testify of Jesus. You and I know that Jesus is the big E on the eye chart—that all of our Christian life centers around his work on the cross. We've studied that even the Holy Spirit spends his ministry pointing to Christ and bringing his teachings to our remembrance. But we often overlook the ways that the whole Bible points to the person and work of Jesus. Instead, we tend to read the Bible, especially the Old Testament, as an incoherent mass of moral lessons.

Let's consider what the whole of Scripture reveals about Jesus. Genesis begins with the story of creation, establishing God as the sole authority over the earth. Man sinned against God, resulting in his eternal separation from God. The rest of the Scriptures reveal God's plan for redeeming his wayward bride, ending in Revelation 21 with the marriage supper uniting Christ and his church for eternity.

How does this story of redemption progress through Scripture? Early in Genesis, shortly after the fall of man, the first blood sacrifices were offered to God. In the stories of Adam and Cain and Abel, we get a foretaste of God's plan to reconcile us once and for all through Jesus' bloody death on the cross. Later, God set Abraham apart to be the father of a great nation and made a covenant with him that all nations would be blessed through Abraham's descendants. The rest of the Old Testament details the history of Abraham's descendants, paying special attention to the line of King David and the right of David's heir to the throne of Israel. Then the New Testament begins with Christ's lineage as a descendant of David, establishing Jesus' legitimate place as the long-foretold Savior of his people.

In light of this overarching theme, most of the Old Testament can be broken into one of three general Christ-centered categories: stories that show God's work to preserve the lineage of Christ; stories that are pictures of the coming Christ; and stories that reinforce our inability to save ourselves and, therefore, our need for salvation through Christ.

Preserved

The first category of Old Testament stories shows God's work to preserve and protect the children of Abraham and especially the line of Christ, the Messiah. Why do we need these stories? The unbroken lineage of the Messiah from Abraham to Jesus was the primary evidence to the Jews of Christ's right to the throne. The story of Joseph in Genesis 37 to 50 falls into this category. Through Joseph, God protects the tiny, newly formed nation of Israel from being wiped out by famine by sending Joseph to Egypt before the

Israelites to win favor with Pharaoh. The book of Esther has a similar theme. It alludes to God's sovereign control over circumstances to put Esther in a place of influence with the king. She was then able to intercede for the Israelites and thwart Haman's plan to annihilate the line of Christ. In the story of Ruth, God works to bring Ruth and Boaz together; they then have a son who is the grandfather of King David. This once again preserves the line of Christ.

Many stories of King David fall into this category. Since Christ's right as Messiah to the throne descends through the line of David (see 2 Samuel 7), David's right to the throne had to be well documented. Many chapters in the book of 1 Samuel are dedicated to assuring those reading it that Samuel was a prophet of God who was obedient and sensitive to God's work in his life. Samuel's qualifications are important because it was he who anointed David to be king. The Old Testament leaves no doubt that Samuel was God's prophet and that David was the king of God's design. Therefore, Christ has a right to the throne as the direct descendant of King David.

Pictures

The second category of stories in the Old Testament could simply be described as pictures of the Messiah. The entire Old Testament sacrificial system is a picture of the sacrifice of the perfect Man, Jesus Christ, dying on the cross. The Psalms and the book of Isaiah give many prophecies of the coming Messiah, revealing details of his appearance and purpose. The story of Ruth and Boaz, as well as that of Hosea and Gomer, are pictures of the Bridegroom buying back the bride and setting her up in an honored position. This is exactly what Christ does for the church throughout the New Testament. The culminating real-life event will be the marriage supper of the Lamb depicted in Revelation 21.

These pictures of Christ helped Old Testament believers to form a mental image of the coming Messiah so that they would recognize him when he came. Consider Philip and Nathanael in John 1:45: "Philip found Nathanael and said to him, 'We have found him of whom Moses in the Law and also the prophets wrote, Jesus of Nazareth, the son of Joseph.'" Before meeting Jesus in person, Philip probably could not have fully articulated all he knew about the Messiah from the Old Testament. But when he finally met the Messiah in person, it clicked. The pieces of the portrait came together, and Philip was confident that this was he. Today, as well, the pictures of Christ in the Old Testament help believers understand Christ's character and function. We know who he is and what he came to do because of those Old Testament illustrations. Pictures of Christ in the Old Testament are fundamental to understanding Christ's essence and role in the New Testament.

Condition

The third category of Old Testament stories reveals the condition of man apart from a Savior and his subsequent need for Jesus. Section after section of the Old Testament shows the temporary nature of the Old Testament sacrificial system, the inability of the Israelites to keep the law on their own, and the sorry condition of God's people when they tried to make decisions for themselves apart from God. Consider the book of Judges, which is perhaps the oddest and most obscure book in the Old Testament. Judges involves stories of horrible crimes: idol worship, rapes, and murders. One story involves a father sacrificing his daughter to God, and another tells of the rape of a concubine whose body was dismembered and spread throughout the land. These are very disturbing accounts of Israel's history. The stories are summed up by the final verse of the book: "In those days there was no king in Israel. Everyone did what was right in his own eyes" (Judges 21:25).

The book of Judges documents the problems that follow when individuals look solely within themselves to determine their best course of action. The book does not include any record that the people punished the one who raped the concubine. No one in the book cries out against the father sacrificing his daughter in a misguided pledge to God. Instead, each of the people committing these acts seems to be doing "what was right in his own eyes." The Israelites, who were supposed to be set apart in a special relationship with God, were deciding for themselves what was right. Because there was no king and no standard of righteousness, they were able to rationalize horrible behavior. Likewise, throughout the ages, those claiming to know Christ have been able to justify behavior that is decidedly not like Christ. The book of Judges serves as a warning to us today that we need the perfect King and his perfect standard of righteousness. *Left on our own and apart from Christ, you and I tend toward very warped views of what is right.* We justify our sinful responses and fool ourselves into living lives that completely dishonor God.

As Christ says, in John 5:39, the Old Testament testifies about him. It testifies of his legitimate right to the throne of Israel through the line of David. It testifies of his earthly ministry and death on the cross through pictures and allusions. It testifies of our depravity apart from him and our need for him as our substitute on the cross. In light of this, it is concerning that while God's redemptive plan is evident in the stories of Joseph, Ruth, Samuel, and David, they are often mishandled by well-meaning preachers who reduce them to a series of children's moral lessons. The stories of Joseph, Ruth, David, Samuel, Jonah, and others are not simply moral lessons. While we can learn from their examples, the main idea is not that we are to emulate their lives or avoid their mistakes. The point of their stories is the transcendent God who moved through their ignorance or knowledge, their obedience or lack thereof, to preserve his people and accomplish his purposes. As Joseph said to his brothers who sold him into slavery, "You meant evil against me, but God meant it for good, to bring it about that many people should be kept alive, as they are today" (Genesis 50:20).

Becoming Like Him

The stories of the Old Testament are much more than mere moral lessons from men of old. Don't reduce 1 and 2 Samuel to a study of the rise and fall of David. Don't read Genesis 37 to 50 simply to learn about Joseph's character traits. Don't merely seek to be like Gideon and Daniel or unlike Jonah and Saul. These stories are ultimately about God. They point to Jesus Christ. Seek to be like him.

According to Romans 8:29, we are predestined to be conformed to the image of Jesus Christ. The examples of Abraham, Joseph, and David are valuable in their reflection of Christ and what they teach us about repentance from sin, but they lose their power when removed from God's gospel purposes and plans. Your personal story will be so different from the circumstances surrounding those Old Testament characters—but your God is the same! He is the common element that allows us to sift through the lives of Old Testament believers and glean truth from them for today. That truth is ultimately centered on the Kinsman-Redeemer foretold throughout the Old Testament, Jesus Christ.

The Bible begins with a divorce and ends with a marriage. The rest of Scripture tells the story of God's plan for buying back his wayward bride. With that picture in mind, the Scriptures, including difficult books like Judges, begin to fit together like pieces of a puzzle or layers of paint on a fine work of art. Read each book with a view of God's eternal plan of salvation, and ask yourself how each Scripture contributes to the canvas of that most beautiful portrait, a redeemed bride sitting with her Bridegroom at the marriage supper of the Lamb.

The Bible Is Sufficient

A key word I think of when I sum up the Scriptures in my mind (if that is even possible) is the word *sufficient*. The Bible is sufficient. It is enough. Remember what Paul said: "All Scripture is breathed out by God and profitable for teaching, for reproof, for correction, and for training in righteousness, that the man of God may be competent, equipped for every good work" (2 Timothy 3:16–17). Wow! It's amazing to think that believers can be completely equipped for everything to which God has called them through Scripture alone. In contrast, the church has been famous for adding to the Scriptures over the years. The Catholic Church does that with no apologies. At least they are honest. But there are also a large number of Protestant groups that have historically claimed that the Bible is their only source for faith and practice but do the same.

Why do many churches add cultural standards to Scripture to come up with a new standard of morality beyond what is stated there? Many groups that say the Bible is their only source for faith and practice have actually added a variety of requirements beyond those specifically given in Scripture. Adding requirements to Scripture is an abuse of Scripture that needs to be addressed boldly, as Christ did (Mark 7:1–13). There, Christ strongly rebukes the Pharisees for "rejecting the commandment of God in order to establish [their] tradition!" (v. 9). This has happened often throughout the history of the church. Leaders elevate human traditions to the level of Scripture and require things of believers that the Bible does not require. The Pharisees did it concerning tithing their spice rack and washing their hands. The Catholic Church did it with issues such as the selling of indulgences in the Middle Ages and with birth control in the twenty-first century. Many denominations and churches have their own traditions that fight with Scripture for supremacy. *There is a lot in Christianity today that is easily defended by human logic but utterly lacking in a biblical foundation.* We must ask ourselves, isn't the Scripture sufficient in its condemnation of sin? Did God forget to mention some sin areas when he inspired the writers of the Word? Is he surprised by the issues facing Christians today, thereby justifying the addition of extra-biblical standards of moral behavior for the church? The Word of God is living and powerful. It transcends cultures, time, and human reasoning. It is as relevant today as it was two thousand years ago. And it is sufficient to thoroughly equip every believer for every good work God has called him to do.

15

How Do We Interact with the Word?

Most of us want to understand the Bible. If you've read this far in this book, chances are you love God and want to know more about him. But many believers, especially Christian women, are not confident in their own personal study of the Word. Does Scripture intimidate you? Are you frustrated by hard-to-understand passages in the Bible?

The Bible definitely presents many hard concepts. What do we do with these things? First, don't be surprised or put off when you don't completely understand a passage. Concerning the hardest biblical truths we try to grasp, the Bible is the only source that explains them exactly right. Although we want to understand all of Scripture, the Bible would not be the eternal, living Word of God if we could get our minds around every concept in it. Do I want a God who is no deeper than I am? Do I want a God who doesn't transcend my ability to reason? I can't even understand the physics of planetary motion, so why should I be surprised that I can't completely dissect and reconcile every piece of the written Word of the Creator of planetary motion?

John Calvin once said that God talks to us like we talk to babies. He uses words we understand, but there is so much meaning behind those words that we cannot yet comprehend. I think of that idea when I talk to my dogs. When I bring my dogs in at night, I make them sit so that I can wipe their feet. The only word I use with them is a strongly toned "sit," repeated often but with little commentary. There is no point in trying to explain to them all of the reasons I need to wipe their feet or how much better it is for them to be free to run around in the house with clean feet. They simply wouldn't understand my explanation, so I use the one word they do understand: "Sit!"

In a much greater fashion, God is working many wonderful things in our lives that are far beyond our ability to understand. His ways are far above our ways (Isaiah 55:9). In a particularly trying time in my life, it seemed that the Lord was simply saying over and over again to me, "Wait!" Looking back at that time, I realize that it was impossible for me to understand the complexities of the issues he was working out for my good and his glory. So he spoke to me with the few words I could understand. "Wait." "Trust." "Obey."

The God who hung the stars in the sky transcends my understanding. However, he is graciously leading me to understand more and more of himself through the Word. Sometimes I read a passage of Scripture that I can't reconcile in my own mind. When that happens, I don't become frustrated that God's ways are above my own. Instead, I consider the psalmist's prayer: "Open my eyes, that I may behold wondrous things out of your law" (Psalm 119:18). His prayer implies that our understanding of the Word depends on God's opening our eyes, which are otherwise blinded to the power and meaning of it. If you read the Word and seem at a loss to figure out the value and meaning, take time to pray earnestly that God would enable you to see his beauty and truth revealed there. Then be thankful that God's ways are above our ways, remembering that the planets still rotate around the sun whether you can document the formulas and explain the physics or not.

The Bible Is the Best Commentary on Itself

In our quest to understand Scripture, remember that no one explains the Bible better than the Bible explains itself. A wise friend once told me, "It's amazing the light that the Bible sheds on the commentaries." I like Bible commentaries; they can be a great help in understanding the Scripture. However, many Bible students seem to rely more on what books say about the Bible than on what the Bible says about itself. No commentary can explain the Bible better than the Bible can explain itself. The message of the Old Testament becomes clear when we study the New Testament and vice versa. The New Testament writers regularly quoted the Old Testament to give their readers insight into their message. Therefore, it is wise to carefully consider each cross-reference within Scripture, for each is like a line connecting the dots in a drawing. In such a drawing, each connection gives a better perspective of the picture until all of the connections are made and the picture is revealed. Similarly, each cross-reference gives a little more insight into the connected, coherent story of God's redemptive plan for man.

Consider the following examples. In each one, do you see the significance of the link between the Old Testament passage and the New Testament's use of it?

- Paul quotes Genesis 15:6 when he explains salvation in Romans 4:3: "For what does the Scripture say? 'Abraham believed God, and it was counted to him as righteousness.'"

- The writer of Hebrews quotes Psalm 45:6 when he presents Jesus in Hebrews 1:8: "But of the Son he says, 'Your throne, O God, is forever and ever, the scepter of uprightness is the scepter of your kingdom.'"
- My all-time favorite New Testament use of the Old Testament is a reference to Isaiah 61:1–3:

> The Spirit of the Lord GOD is upon me,
>> because the LORD has anointed me
> to bring good news to the poor;
>> he has sent me to bind up the brokenhearted,
> to proclaim liberty to the captives,
>> and the opening of the prison to those who are bound;
> to proclaim the year of the LORD's favor,
>> and the day of vengeance of our God;
>> to comfort all who mourn;
> to grant to those who mourn in Zion—
>> to give them a beautiful headdress instead of ashes,
> the oil of gladness instead of mourning,
>> the garment of praise instead of a faint spirit;
> that they may be called oaks of righteousness,
>> the planting of the LORD, that he may be glorified.

I always thought that was an encouraging passage. But is it reality? How is God going to "bind up the brokenhearted"? There was a tremendous amount of mourning in Israel after that passage was written, and there is an awful lot of misery in Israel today. However, it all made perfect sense when I read Christ's quotation of that passage in Luke 4:16–21:

> He came to Nazareth, where he had been brought up. And as was his custom, he went to the synagogue on the Sabbath day, and he stood up to read. And the scroll of the prophet Isaiah was given

to him. He unrolled the scroll and found the place where it was written,

> "The Spirit of the Lord is upon me,
>> because he has anointed me
>> to proclaim good news to the poor.
> He has sent me to proclaim liberty to the captives
>> and recovering of sight to the blind,
>> to set at liberty those who are oppressed,
> to proclaim the year of the Lord's favor."
> And he rolled up the scroll and gave it back to the at-
> tendant and sat down. And the eyes of all in the
> synagogue were fixed on him. And he began to say to
> them, "Today this Scripture has been fulfilled in your
> hearing."

I got goose bumps the first time I read that last phrase, "Today this Scripture has been fulfilled in your hearing." Connecting the dots between those two passages and seeing Christ as the fulfillment of this Old Testament promise was a very important moment for me in understanding the relationship between Christ, the Old Testament, and the New Testament. Nobody explains the Bible better than the Bible explains itself. So don't ignore cross-references when you are studying the Word.

Get into It!

Let me end this chapter with a word of encouragement. Many of us don't *feel* like we get much out of reading the Bible. Our reaction is to cop out; we'll listen to what others say about Scripture in books or sermons but avoid studying it for ourselves. Certainly the preaching of the Word is a primary way that God speaks to his children. So take advantage of all the opportunities you have to hear the preaching of the Word. However, you cannot abandon your own study of the Bible and expect a healthy relationship with the Father, Son, and Holy Spirit. The written Word of God is his *logos*—his written expression of his character and purposes. The written Word alone is the hammer that breaks the heart of stone and the sword that pierces our thoughts. You cannot be thoroughly equipped for service to God apart from personal study of his written Word.

I have often heard others talk of the power of spending thirty minutes alone with God each morning before the day gets started. I have always admired that. I want to do that. However, when I was younger and actually had the time to do that, I never had the self-discipline. And now, as a mother of two small boys, I don't even have the time. But recently I made a startling discovery—reading my Bible isn't nearly as difficult an endeavor as I had made it out to be. It doesn't require a substantial amount of time in a quiet and private location. The only requirement is that I make it a priority. Every morning it takes me fifteen minutes or so to get my young boys breakfast and clean clothes. Then, when we are all settled for a few minutes, I usually run to check my e-mail. It finally dawned on me, by the Holy Spirit's prompting, that I could read my Bible during that first breathable time in the morning. It does not matter if the boys are watching cartoons in the same room. And the sweet taste of the Word during those first relatively quiet moments of the morning makes a profound impact on the rest of my day.

Maybe you have the time and discipline to spend thirty minutes (or whatever) in quiet, private study. But many more of us use the demands of our stage of life as an excuse against any Bible study. This should not be so. The Bible says that faith comes by hearing the Word (Romans 10:17). The letters to the New Testament churches were originally read to the congregations orally. For us today, a good use of our time may be to put the Bible on our iPod or CD player as we wash dishes, fold laundry, take a shower, or drive to work. Many days, it is hard to find the time to get into the Word, but there are still many ways to allow the Word to get into us.

Where are you in your study of the Word? Do you tend toward what others say about it through Christian books rather than reading the Word for yourself? What do you believe about the power of Scripture? Do you think that power applies to you? If you want to approach the Bible on your own but are intimidated by its depth and density, I suggest starting in the Gospel of Luke. There you can read simply of the life of Christ. Luke includes several connections to the Old Testament that will give you insight into the overall connectedness of Scripture. Best of all, when I read Luke, I keep getting surprised by Jesus. "I can't believe he said that! How did I miss that the last time I read Luke? I've never heard anyone preach on this passage!" God's Word is living and breathing, and, given the chance, it will cut you open with amazing clarity.

Conclusion

We have reached the close of this book, and yet I could say so much more about God the Father, God the Son, God the Spirit, prayer, and Bible study. I hope you take away a couple of key ideas from this work. First and foremost, you cannot be equipped for wise daily living apart from knowing the character and work of God, and the Word is the primary way God reveals himself to us. Before time began, God determined to adopt you into his family. Believers are now indwelt with the Holy Spirit and supernaturally connected to Christ. Because of Christ's payment for our sins on the cross, we have a real relationship with God with full access to his presence. Prayer and Bible study are the outworking of this relationship, the key ways in which we communicate to our Father, Counselor, and Bridegroom.

Though we've covered many topics in this short work, we have only touched the surface of each. My hope is that your appetite has been whetted and that you will continue your own earnest study of him. Though we spend a lifetime pursuing knowledge of God, we will have much more to learn of his grandeur and glory when we finally see him face-to-face in heaven. Let us close with Paul's prayer for the believers in Ephesus, which is also my prayer for each of us:

> For this reason I bow my knees before the Father, from whom every family in heaven and on earth is named, that according to the riches of his glory he may grant you to be strengthened with power through his Spirit in your inner being, so that Christ may dwell in your hearts through faith—that you, being rooted and grounded in love, may have strength to comprehend with all the saints what is the breadth and length and height and depth, and to know the love of Christ that surpasses knowledge, that you may be filled with all the fullness of God. Now to him who is able to do far more abundantly than all that we ask or think, according to the power at work within us, to him be glory in the church and in Christ Jesus throughout all generations, forever and ever. Amen. (Ephesians 3:14–21)

Notes

Chapter 1: Why Should I Care?

1. *The American Heritage Dictionary of the English Language,* 4th ed., s.v. "theology."

Chapter 2: What Is Faith?

1. James Strong, *The New Strong's Exhaustive Concordance of the Bible* (Nashville: Thomas Nelson, 1990), s.v. "YHWH."

2. Ibid., s.v. "Hâyâh."

3. C. S. Lewis, *The Weight of Glory* (New York: HarperCollins, 2001), 26.

Chapter 3: Faith Works!

1. James Strong, *The New Strong's Exhuastive Concordance of the Bible* (Nashville: Thomas Nelson, 1990), s.v. "ma'al."

2. Ibid., s.v. "oligopistos."

Chapter 8: Our Father Disciplines Us

1. *The American Heritage Dictionary*, 4th ed., s.v. "discipline."

Chapter 9: God Is Our Savior, Example, and Bridegroom

1. James Strong, *The New Strong's Exhaustive Concordance of the Bible* (Nashville: Thomas Nelson, 1990), s.v. "kenoō."

Chapter 10: We Are Connected to Jesus and Find Our Identity in Him

1. James Strong, *The New Strong's Exhaustive Concordance of the Bible* (Nashville: Thomas Nelson, 1990), s.v. "menō."

Chapter 11: God Is Our Help

1. For further study on subordination in the Trinity, see "1 Corinthians 11," http://www.cbmw.org/resources/articles/WareETS2006.pdf.

2. WordNet 2.0., http://dictionary.reference.com (accessed September 21, 2006).

Chapter 13: Prayer Is Our Means of Conversing with God

1. Wayne Grudem, *Systematic Theology* (Grand Rapids, MI: Zondervan, 1995), 864.